LIVING BEYOND LIMITATIONS EVERY DAY

Twelve Profound Principles on How to Live Beyond Your Limitations Every Day

Kennedy King Odimba

Copyright © 2020 Kennedy King Odimba
All rights reserved
First Edition

Fulton Books, Inc.
Meadville, PA

Published by Fulton Books 2020

ISBN 978-1-64654-097-6 (paperback)
ISBN 978-1-64654-098-3 (digital)

Printed in the United States of America

Doing What Others Say Can't Be Done

I want to dedicate this book to my Lord and personal Savior Jesus Christ for making this abstract concept a reality and to all those individuals who will not settle for less than they can be.

I am profoundly grateful for writers and speakers who have influence my life and thought over the years.

Contents

Foreword 9
Acknowledgment 11
Introduction 13
Principle One: Picture, Venture, and Capture (PVC) 17
Principle Two: Overcoming the Fear Syndrome 24
Principle Three: The Law of Courage 30
Principle Four: Understanding the Purpose of Life 36
Principle Five: The Law of Preparation 42
Principle Six: Change Your Perception 49
Principle Seven: Change Your Priority 54
Principle Eight: Attitude Is Everything 59
Principle Nine: The Power of Determination 65
Principle Ten: The Power of Decision 73
Principle Eleven: The Law of Attraction 83
Principle Twelve: Take Action 91
Reference and Resources 95

Foreword

Acknowledgment

Writing a book is a bit like building a house, and it takes a lot of refining processes. I feel greatly blessed by God to share this profound ideas with you my generation.

I appreciate each person who has contributed in one way on the other to the realization of this lofty dream.

First I would like to thank some special individuals who have really influenced my life positively through their books and seminars: to my father in the Lord, Pastor Tommy Tommy, the founder and president of all blessed Christian Church in Owerri, Nigeria; Rev. Chris Oyakhilome, founding president of Believers Loveword Incorporated headquartered in Lagos, Nigeria; Pastor Joel Osteen, founder of Lakewood Church in Houston, Texas, USA; best-selling authors and speakers Les Brown, Anthony Robins, Brain Tracy, and many others whose books and audio messages has helped shape my life.

Special thanks will also go to the editorial team for believing in this project and to go the extra mile to make sure that it happened.

To my friends, Uchulor Chinedu Noble, Talitha Jackson, for their friendship and professional advice; heartfelt thanks will go to my lovely parents, Mr. and Mrs. Julius Odimba, for their moral support and prayers; lastly, but certainly not the least, to my personal mentor and coach, Renee Bob, and to all those individuals who have directly or indirectly influence the realization of this project, may God bless you all.

Introduction

Empowering people to realize that they determine the outcome of their own lives is not always easy. In fact it's often an overwhelming venture. Over the years I have wondered about what really make the difference in people's life, what is it that really differentiate the poor from the rich.

This dilemma and some of my personal life experiences was what gave birth to this book. We all have dreams and certain targets that we want to attain in life, but it takes some certain level of discipline, acknowledging, and applying some life principles to be able to live our dreams.

Too many people fail in life because of the limited information available to them. We live in an information age; the more information you can access, the further you can advance in your chosen field of endeavor. In other words, seeking profound information is one of the fundamental steps in building a successful life.

If you want to cook, you study cooking, and you follow the rules and principles regarding the combining of ingredients and preparation that has been found to work successfully in the past. You would not think to add or subtract key ingredients and expect the dish that you are preparing to taste the same as if you followed the proven pattern. In the same token, you would not expect to succeed in life and start living beyond your limitations by violating the essential laws and principles which has been discovered and practiced by some of the most successful people in our world today.

It's therefore of utmost importance to understand that your success in life will largely be dependent on discovering and applying what works and not just wishing and hoping for miracles.

Universal laws and principles are similar to telephone numbers. If you dial the right numbers, you will definitely get through to the right person that you desire to talk to.

If you are genius, smart, and intelligent, you won't get through if you omit any one of the digits of the numbers. This analogy further confirms the law of cause and effect propounded by Aristotle so many years ago, which states that "in every effect there is an equal and opposite cause" which literally means that if you do what others did and succeed, you will also succeed.

Time and time again, I have been obsessed with the questions: What is the difference between the rich and the poor? Why is it that people who are from very humble background with no connection or even support still manage to rise to the top of their carriers in a very short period of time?

The more I ask these questions, the more I discover that there are some intangible successful values, attitudes, and approaches to life that sets us apart from our peers. These same values are some of the key ingredients that determine how far we go in life.

The purpose of this book, therefore, is to help you understand this values or principles and how you can immediately apply them to your own life for a triumphant change and advancement in your life.

In fact this book is fundamentally aimed at pulling you, the reader, out of any shackles of limitation, fear, and despair facing you right now. In your journey through this book, you will uncover twelve profound laws on how to provoke success in any area of your life.

I wrote this book out of my dissatisfaction on how poorly individuals perform in life without realizing and utilizing the powers, potentials, skills, and ideals given to them by God. Oftentimes these problems are caused by what I call self-limiting beliefs, a mind-set of unworthiness, fear, low self-esteem, etc. This book is a wake-up call to the twenty-first-century youth that there is more to their life than they are currently expressing.

By the inspiration given to me by God seven years ago, today I am confident to assure you that if you will sincerely and thoughtfully read this book, you will see self-achieving, greater results with less effort, and this will ultimately lead you to experiencing a more positive and productive life. The Bible recorded in the Book of Hosea (4:6), "My people are destroyed for lack of knowledge."

Thomas Hobbes, an English philosopher in the seventeenth century, opined that knowledge is power. This book, therefore, will be, to the reader, an invaluable source of uncommon knowledge on how to leave and prosper mostly in this time of high competition and rapid change. Hence the more you align your life to the principles and values that you will discover in the pages of this book, the more happiness and success you will begin to experience.

And you will ultimately come to the realization that there is no limit to what you can achieve in life. Your heavenly Father has wired you with unlimited potentials and greatness, so welcome on board as I take you on a step-by-step approach on how you can start unleashing every greatness that is within you, not minding how life has treated you in the past or how many times you have failed. I believe that if you can look up, you can stand up. Say yes to life.

Principle One

Picture, Venture, and Capture (PVC)

Whatever the mind of man can conceive and believe, it can achieve.
—Napoleon Hill

The questions what do I really want in life, who do I want to be, what on earth am here to accomplish, why was I born at a particular time like this, etc. are some of the most fundamental questions that has been asked by some of the greatest philosophers and scientist over the years. Which has led to many theories and discoveries that has continually advance the course of humanity and will continue to be the guiding light to future inventions and discoveries. That is why I believe that problem and challenges are very vital in the prosperity of humankind. What this means is that we cannot have a problem-free life, we are either running toward something or something is running toward us.

    Therefore facing and overcoming your challenges on a daily basis is a proof that you are still worthy to be here. Hence anyone who will tell you that he has never experience pain or failure in their life, may have not really tried anything worthwhile in his or her life before. So the problem of humanity is never going to be exhaustive, it is a continual working process. This book, however, is a way to give or recommend some proven principles on how to thrive successfully through this challenges and limitations on a one-at-a-time basis. In other words while the search for how, what, when, and the why of human problems possess a limitation to the progress of humankind, it is also a necessary ingredient in the advancement of ideas and imaginations that will lead to more and more simplified ways on how to solve future challenges that lies ahead. It is never exhaustive.

Hence on this chapter, we will be looking at the concept of PVC, which simply means picture, venture, and capture, as one the key ways to give answers to this dilemma. Firstly, what is a picture? I simply define a picture as a visual representation of an object past, present, or future. In other words, it matters what kind of mental representation you have in your mind, that is negative or positive. All worthwhile achievement begins from your mental representations of things whether past, present, or future. That is why the Bible teaches in the Book of Romans 12:2 saying, "Be ye transformed by the renewal of your mind." This means an active participation in changing your thoughts and mental representation of things in your heart. In other words, fill your heart with positive thoughts because whatever you see in your heart is what you will eventually have in material reality. One of my favorite English quotes says, "If you can change a man's thought pattern, you have unconsciously change his entire approach to life" (Anonymous).

So many of us are stuck and stagnated in life not because of our location, past experiences, or economic policies of the government of our countries but because of our mental representation of what is possible for us. We have limited ourselves with what I may call self-impose limitation, a feeling of unworthiness, negative presuppositions, and lack of courage to venture into our dreams.

I write this book to submit to you that you have greatness within you. There is literally nothing you cannot accomplish if you put your potentials, energy, and focus on it, but you must begin to develop and create the right mental picture for your preferable future. I may not know the level of your challenges or uncertainties that you are facing right now in your life, but one thing I'm certain about is that you can stop focusing your mind on what is wrong and who is wrong and start looking ahead with a positive mind-set coupled with taking courageous decisions toward your objectives with the help of the supreme being who is the creator of the universe, God.

You will begin to accomplish more with less effort, and soon your lost happiness will be restored. Time and time again we fail in life because we make poor evaluation of the challenges that we face on daily basis. In other words, poor evaluation leads to a poor life, thoughtful and proper evaluation leads to a rich life; learn to look at any challenge facing you right now with a possibility mind-set because if you can see beyond it, you can leave above it. It all starts in your mind; a positive mental state of mind is the beginning of all worthwhile achievements.

You have to wake up every morning with the mind-set of positivity, say to yourself that it's possible. Rephrase words like, it's possible that I can leave my dreams, it's possible that I can start my own business, it's possible that I can get to the top of my field, and before long your heart will be obsessed with the positive vibes required to pull you beyond limits. It was Napoleon Hill that said, "There are no limitations to the mind except those that we acknowledge."

Now here is my point. Begin to develop the mental pictures of what you want to be, do, have, and accomplish in the years to come because if you can picture it and venture in to it, you will capture it. Put in another way, conceive it, believe it, and you will accomplish it. It makes no difference how big or impossible your dreams and objective are, it depends in your ability to believe in yourself. The fact is that you are smarter, more powerful, and intelligent than you are currently expressing right now. All you need to do is to push beyond limits, step out of your comfort zone.

It was William J. H. Boetcker, who said, "You can succeed if nobody else believes it, but you will never succeed if you don't believe in yourself." All worthwhile achievements spring up from self-belief, a belief that I can make it happen for me. We live in a very fast-paced and competitive world. There are a lot of discoveries and inventions coming up. The world as we have it today has become a global village, people are learning and developing new skills in order to remain relevant in their various field of endeavors.

If we must, therefore, compete favorably with our peers today, we must consciously begin to develop some kind of attitude, goals, visions, and the needed courage required to venture in to the pictures in our heart. The term picture, venture, and capture (PVC) was a concept I developed so many years ago in one of my quiet moments, and over the years I have practiced and applied this principle in my own personal life. The more I understand and apply this principle, the more I accomplish greater things with great rewards. Author and writer, John C. Mason, opined visualize success and you will succeed, visualize failure and you will fail.

The fact is that whatever you see in our world today was once a picture in someone's heart, but the distinguishing factor was that they had the courage to venture into those pictures in their heart to be able to make them to what we'll call inventions today—the cars, computers, airplanes etc.—that we are all enjoying today. We're all at one point a mere pictures or ideas in the inventor's mind. Here is my point, we must begin to develop the required courage needed to turn our ideas and dreams into reality. We all want to achieve greater things in life, we all have some ideas or pictures of what we want to accomplish in life. But the challenge for most people has always been clarity and the ability to focus on one thing until it is accomplished. The fact is that there is nothing you cannot accomplish if you decide to.

A writer once said that nothing can stop a human will which will stake even its existence for what he wants in life. Where do you see yourself in two years from now, five years from now, ten years from now? Many of us cannot give satisfactory answers to this question. In other words, the picture in your heart is like a road map to your preferred destination in life. The Bible teaches us that God has promised to give us the desires of our heart.

The problem with many of us believers today is that we don't even have clear desires or some specific set goals of what we want to achieve. We are just living every day wishing and experimenting our lives on different things. This, therefore, becomes a challenge to our Creator because he cannot even figure out any clear cut, specific desire in our heart to work with. There is power in picture; the fact is that whatever you see in our world today was once a picture at one point in someone's mind.

It is of utmost important, therefore, that you begin to develop a beautiful picture for your future because if you can see it in your spirit, you can bring it to material reality. Best-selling author and speaker, Les Brown, said in one of his numerous quotes that the worst thing that can happen to an individual is not being able to achieve his goals, but the worse thing is not having any goal to pursue. Imagine a soccer team playing a competition without a goalpost.

They will just be running around in a vicious circle without anything to show for their effort. Author Anthon St. Maarten made a powerful statement when he said, and I quote, "Dare to dream! If you did not have the capability to make your wildest wishes come true, your mind would not have the capacity to conjure such ideas in the first place."

There is no limitation on what you can potentially achieve, except for the limitations you choose to impose on your own imagination. My point, therefore, in PVC simply means that you should visualize a picture of your preferable future, capture it with precision, focus on it and make it specific enough to be able to interpret it to someone else, then develop the courage to venture into it. And consistently act on it until it is accomplished.

One of my favorite verse in the Bible that has changed my mind-set over the years is Philippians 4.13. It says, "I can do all things through Christ that strengthens me." I want to submit to you that you have the skills, potentials, ideas, and the ability to turn your dreams into reality; all you need is to venture in to whatever you want with courage because where there is a will there is way.

If you can see yourself becoming that engineer, doctor, actor, musician, lawyer, etc., you can be it. The three basic steps is to picture it, venture in to it, and capture it with courage. The Book of Proverbs 23:7 says that as a man thinketh in his heart so is he. In other words, if you can think it, you can be it.

Hence I understand that many of us has not been able to act on our dreams because of what I call the "what-if factor." Oftentimes we are faced with the negative questions like what if it doesn't work out, what if no one support me, what if my friends laugh at me. But the fact is that you can never know what you can do until you try.

Author and writer Robert M. Pirsig confirmed this when he said, and I quote, "It's so hard when contemplated in advance, and so easy when you do it." The fact to note here is that beginning is half done; the moment you develop the courage to take the first step, all other things will begin to fall in place to support its realization. Act on that idea, work on that skill, venture into that project. There is no limit to want what you can achieve if only you can see beyond your limitation. You can leave beyond your limitation.

Author and motivational speaker Les Brown made a powerful statement when he said, "If you can look up you can stand up." I challenge you today to take a bold step toward that goal or task that you have set for yourself because you have been equipped with the ideas, skills, and ability to accomplish it even before you conceptualize the dream. You have what it takes to go for it. You have to realize that no one else is going to sing your own music, no one is going to make your own invention that was given to you, or write your own book. It was given to you by God, and only you can bring it to reality.

The moment you take the first bold step toward it, the resources, materials, personnel, and all other connections that will support its realization will begin to show up. It was Albert Einstein, one of the greatest scientists of the twentieth century that said, "Imagination is more important than knowledge." What this means, therefore, is that while your knowledge can take you from point A to point B, imagination can take you to wherever you want to go in life. In fact the determining factor between your now and your next two years, five years, ten years, etc. is largely depended on the imagination and pictures in your heart. The Bible in the Book of Proverbs 23:7 says, "As he thinketh his heart so is he." In other words, if you can imagine it, you can bring it in to reality. There is no limit.

Key Important Points to Note from the Foregoing Chapter

1. All worthwhile accomplishments begin with a positive, clear mental picture.

2. You can have, do, and become anything you want to be by venturing into your dreams without fear, doubt, or hesitancy
3. You have all the skills, power, and ability to turn your dreams into reality if only you can believe in yourself.
4. Whatever idea you can conceptualize in your mind and consistently act and believe in it, with the help of the supreme being, God, you will eventually bring it to materialization.

Principle Two

Overcoming the Fear Syndrome

You will never know what you can do until you try.
—Kennedy King

Have you noticed that there are people you know who are literally at the same place today as they were five years ago? Hence they are gifted, healthy, and very intelligent, but they have been stagnated in life due to fear and lack of confidence to act on their God-given potentials and ideas. They are just standing still in life.

And oftentimes these things are caused by their presupposition and self-limiting beliefs that have been contracted from past experiences, peer groups, and fear of the unknown. Over the years, I have come to this one conclusion that our life depends on many things but mostly on our ability to believe in ourselves. There is literally nothing the human mind cannot accomplish if it takes its capability and focus on it. Ralf Waldo Emerson said, "It is impossible for a man to be cheated by anyone but himself." Here is my point, gain control over your mind or it will gain control over you; your imagination is the creator of your future.

There is no limitation to the heart except the ones we acknowledge. In other words, visualize failure and you will fail, visualize success and you will succeed; it all boils down to what you focus on. The term fear has been defined by some authors from the acronym F.E.A.R., meaning false evidence appearing real. A lot of folks has been stagnated in life due to some false and unrealistic evidence of why they should not venture in to their dreams. For example, using Mr. A as an analogy. Mr. A tried it, it did not work for him, therefore it will not work for me too. I do not have the connection, nobody in our family has done that before, I am not smart enough, I don't have a college degree. All this and many more are some of the self-imposed beliefs that has limited some of us from reaching our ultimate goal in life.

That's why I'm putting together ideas and principles in this book to challenge you to step into your fear with courage because your victory lies in the other side of your fear. Don't let past experiences, friends, or even your family opinion deter you from venturing into your dreams. Your creator has equipped you with all the abilities, skills, ideas, and even resources that are required to bring your dreams into reality. All that is required from you, therefore, is to act on it without any form of doubt or hesitancy, and all other things will begin to fall in place. The moment you make the first move, all other ideas you need will begin to spring up naturally. The difficulty for many folks often lies in taking the first step.

Dr. Robert H. Schuller, pastor of the Crystal Cathedral, has this to say about fear: Faith is often called a leap. Faith is leaping across the gaps between the known and the unknown, the proven and the unproven, the actual and the possible, the grasp and the reach.

There is always a chasm between where you are right now and where you are going—by faith make the leap forward. What lies ahead? Tomorrow? Next week? Next month? Next year? Beyond this life? Believe in faith, believe in God, believe in tomorrow. Take the leap of faith.

From the foregoing we can fully understand that it takes the leap of faith and belief to overcome our fears. In other words, we must learn to walk by faith and not by sight when it comes to stepping into our fears, that is having a belief there is something inside of you that is more superior to your circumstances, call it a supreme being, unseen falsies of the universe, or God. The fact remains that you will literally be amazed by the result and outcome. You will begin to produce as you begin to act on your fears with faith, courage, and a sense of guaranteed success even before you take the first step, hence.

This statement brings us back to the reality of the previous chapter where we have established that the mind thinks in pictures not in words. That is whatever we vividly picture and desire in our heart will eventually become a reality, in time.

In other words, if you can think it, you can have it; it makes no difference how impossible it may look from the unset or the level of resources available to you right now rather it's in your decision to venture in to your plans with boldness and a positive mind-set that will make the difference. Don't let questions like how will I make it happen, what if nobody give me the support that I need, what if I fail, etc. stop you from acting on those precious ideas that pop into your mind on daily basis.

In fact there is a recent research by a psychologist, Bruce Davis, PhD, that an average individual receives not less than 50,000 to 70,000 ideas per day, but the sad thing is that most of us has ended up not acting on this ideas due do what I call the "what-if factor." That is we have short-circuited our own progress by our own self-imposed limitation. This confirms the famous quote of Napoleon Hill that says, "There is no limitation to the human mind except the ones we acknowledge."

The Bible in the Book of Mark 9:23 recorded a very profound statement that confirms the powers of believing in ourselves, and it reads, "Jesus said to him, 'If you can believe, all things are possible to him who believes.'" Now take a close look at the verse again, did you notice the word "to him that believes"?

In other words, it makes no difference what kind of fear you are facing in your life right now if only you can believe in yourself. With the help of God, you will overcome every challenge that has been limiting your personal and career goals, and gradually you will start living above all your limitations. Again you have to understand that fear is the number one obstacle that stops people from achieving their goals. It doesn't matter how talented, brilliant, or smart they are, that is why I see this chapter as the most important phase of this work. The moment you overcome your fear, there is literally no power in the universe that can stop your dreams from materialization. But, hey, I know it's sometimes scary.

When we are facing adversities, it can even feel like you are coming to the end of your rope, but believe me, whatever that cannot kill you will eventually make you stronger. I want you to understand that you are stronger than what you think, you are far more powerful than you can ever imagine.

You have the power to turn your ideas in to concrete reality. The fact that people you may know or have read about were able to turn their own ideas into reality is enough evidence to prove that you, too, can live your dreams.

A friend of mine once told me a story of her auntie who was afraid to get on the airplane for a business trip simply because there was a plane crash the previous week on the same route. She was about to embark on and a friend of hers was involved in the crash. This experience beclouded her mind with negative impression and imaginations that accumulated into her believing that she might be involved in a similar incident if she embarks on the trip while in reality it doesn't necessarily mean that you will experience an accident or any sort of negative occurrence just because someone you know has experienced it. In other words, the fear that was generated by her negative mental pictures ended up denying her of a multimillion dollar trip that she was about to make for her trade.

Too many times we let our negative imaginations of things that are not really after our lives stop us from making progress in life. We sort of limit ourselves by magnifying fears of objects or events that might not really cause us any harm. You and I must realize that our success in life will largely be dependent on stepping in to our fears and facing it head on. If you keep on procrastinating about venturing in to your dreams because of fear and doubt about the future and not acting on your goals, what will happen is that your fear will eventually gain control over you. So here is my point, gain control over your fears or your fears will gain control over you. By now I know you don't want to be the one who is leaving his fears instead of leaving his dreams. It was Bruce Barton that said, "Nothing splendid has ever been achieved except by those who dared believe that something inside them was superior to circumstances."

Friend, I want to submit to you that you are stronger than any challenge that is facing you right now. This goes further to confirm what I said earlier in this chapter that we are more powerful, smarter, and intelligent than we are currently expressing. All we need is to believe in our God-given abilities and ultimately utilize them to chart the course of our lives.

Resolve today to confront your fears, make an absolute decision and commitment that no matter what happens in your life, you will leave your dreams. And as you begin to act boldly and courageously toward your goals, nothing will be impossible to you, and soon you will become a positive influence on anyone that comes around you.

Therefore, I want you to start taking action right now. What goal or objective have you been putting off to act on due to the fear of failure? The living Bible version of Ecclesiastes 11:4 reads, "If you wait for perfect conditions, you will never get anything done. Here is my point, eliminate all the reasons and excuses that have been stopping you from taking immediate action. It was Herbert Spencer that said, "The great aim of education is not knowledge but action." What do you want to achieve in your personal life? Where do you want to be, say two years or five years from now? Do you want to be rich? I want to submit to you that it is possible, but you have to start the work and take the risk that may be involved along the way. It was John Newman that said, "Calculation never made a hero. Every person has a chance to improve himself, but some just don't believe in taking chances. Being destined for greatness requires that you take risks and confront great hazards."

Here is my point, if you ever going to see your dreams come through, you have to resolve today to start taking chances. Get rid of procrastination and indecision and step into your fears. Then the progress will begin.

Key Important Points to Note from the Foregoing Chapter

1. Your success in any endeavor will largely be dependent on your ability to step in to your fears.
2. Make an absolute commitment that nothing can stop you from reaching your goals.
3. You have the ability, power, and intelligence that require you to face any challenge and overcome.
4. Whatever you can imagine in your heart and continuously act upon with courage, you will accomplish.
5. Your fears are false evidences that seems real to your imaginations; change your mental pictures and get rid of your fears.

Principle Three

The Law of Courage

> Courage is rightly considered the foremost of the
> virtues, for upon it, all others depend.
> —Winston Churchill

The development of courage, self-confidence, boldness, and the will to venture into your dreams in the means of uncertainties and unpleasant circumstances are perhaps some of the most important quality of success anyone should aspire to obtain. This is one quality that separates winners from losers. We live in a very competitive generation; there are a lot of discoveries and innovations going on in different fields of endeavors. It will, therefore, take the development of courage to compete favorably with the challenges that lies ahead in business, academics, politics, even in our day-to-day family decisions. We need courage to navigate our way successfully through life challenges.

In other words, anywhere you see significant success, someone must have been taking some courageous decision to obtain it. The *Oxford Advanced Learner's Dictionary* defines the term courage as the ability to face extreme danger and difficulties without fear, that is the ability to maintain a positive mind-set in the presence of pain or adversities.

Courageous people are those kinds of individuals who never accept that something is impossible. They never take no for an answer. They are always ready to go the extra mile to try one more time, to push beyond limits. Throughout history, our world has continually been shaped by men and women who dared believed that something inside of them was more superior to their circumstances.

Dr. Viktor Frankl was incarcerated in the Nazi prison camp during World War II. They killed his family and burn his manuscript on logo therapy. But he said to himself, "I can still lead in something. I cannot determine when I will be beaten, but I can decide to maintain a positive attitude. I cannot determine when I will be kicked, but I can still determine the direction of my life after I have been kicked." That's the spirit of courage expressed by Dr. Viktor Frankl.

It takes the power of courage to stay focused on your goals in the face of pain and difficulties. The question is not whether you are going to be knocked down by challenges on your way to realizing your ambitions in life, you will; the big deal, however, is refusing to stay down. It was Les Brown that said, "When life knocks you down, try to land on your back. Because if you can look up, you can get up."

Two men are short down in Vietnam and imprisoned in the infamous Hoa Lo prison. They were isolated, chained to cement slabs, and continuously beaten by rusty shackles and tortured for information. Yet although these men are receiving the same torture and abuse, they formed radically different beliefs from their experience. One man decided that his life is over; in order to avoid any additional pain, he commits suicide and die.

The other remained calm in courage and pull himself out of the brutalizing experience. This story once again is a demonstration of the power of the human spirit. I like the old English proverb that says, "Where there's a will, there's a way." In other words, it takes the will, persistence, and courage to surmount any obstacle that is facing you right now. It makes no difference how small or big it may seem, if you can persist and stay in courage, you will triumph.

Here is my point, make a courageous commitment today to stay positive and consistent in that dream you are pursuing, not minding how many times you have been rejected or denied, not minding how risky or impossible it may appear to you right now. It all depends on your mental pictures. If you persist in faith, your fears will give up their holds over your mind. You have to understand that you are stronger than whatever challenge that is facing you right now; all it takes, however, is the belief in yourself and the momentum of courage to overcome.

I want to challenge you to step out with boldness toward the direction of your highest goals. It makes no difference how many times they have said no to you or how many times you have had the word impossible. There is this story about my college years that has inspired my perception about life and my progress for the last six years now; it thought me that the word impossible is only an opinion, not a reality. Sometime six years ago, I finished my graduate program in philosophy from my state university back in my country of Nigeria.

I started doing my final clearance to enable me to qualify to go for a compulsory one-year service for my country, Nigeria, which is basically known as NYSC. It is a one-year program that is set aside for all university graduate who have completed their degree program in various universities around the country. Normally on the process, the school have to screen all your documents, making sure you have paid all debts and academic fees that have not been paid to the school and that you have the right credentials that will enable your successful graduation by the school registrar.

I went through the offices of the head of my department, the head of my faculty, office in charge of sports and recreation, student union, security, and finally I was left with the office of the registrar to authenticate my credentials. So on my first day to her office, when I got on her desk to see her, there was a problem. After she has gone through my credentials, she came up with a shocking discovery that the result I used to gain admission in to the university four years ago was no longer approved by the university governing board, that she will not be able to sign my credentials, that it was a new policy that started that year, and that as a matter of fact I will not be able to graduate that year until I'm able to maybe provide a new result that is accepted by the board or until the policy is reverse in a future date. But at the moment it's not possible for her to graduate me.

So I left her office that day feeling hopeless and mentally drained. The next day, I was reading an article where I came across this quote by author and speaker Les Brown. It said, "Don't let someone else's opinion of you become your reality." And right at that moment, there was a change in my mental state, so I embark on a three-day praying and fasting, asking God to change the mind of the registrar to work for my good. I had only four days left to meet up with the graduation deadline for that year.

After my prayers, I decided to write a letter to the university governing board to appeal for a consideration to let me graduate since my admission into the university was authentic as at the time I gained admission four years ago, but to my shock, I got a reply that same day that it was not possible for them to go against the new school policy, that I have to wait till further notice. But I refused to give up, instead I choose to stay positive.

I went back the next day to visit some senior professors in my faculty, appealing for them to speak up my case in their next board meeting, but on each of my attempt to speak with them, the reply I got was that it's not possible, yet I kept pushing. All I kept hearing was the word "impossible." I had this word approximately ten times from different professors, but I remained positive that I will graduate that same year.

So on the last day of the clearance, I got up very early around, 5:00 a.m., prayed for one hour, and wrote a second letter of appeal, however this time, to the registrar herself. I packaged it in brown envelop, dressed up on my suit, sprayed my perfume, shave my beard, and was feeling optimistic about my decision to revisit her office one more time. So I stepped out with a renewed courage and boldness, with a mentality that I cannot be denied or rejected this time. I got into her office, working with a bold smile and confidence. I greeted her, "Good morning, madam"—sounding as if I'm seeing her for the first time—"I am here to submit my credentials for my final clearance." And immediately she smiled back at me, took my credentials, went carefully through it again, but this time with more speed and little or no attention to what is wrong or what is right. She smiled all through and signed my credentials and congratulated me.

It sounded to me as if I was in a dream, but it was actually a reality. This experience thought me an unforgettable lesson of my life. In fact it has shaped and will continue to shape my perception about life and about what is possible for me, and I hope it will do same to you too. I challenge you to hang on tough and follow your dreams with courage and determination. I like the line that reads "Nothing in this world can take the place of persistence. Talent will not; nothing is more common than unsuccessful men with talent. Genius will not; unrewarded genius is almost a proverb. Education will not; the world is full of educated derelicts. Persistence and determination alone are omnipotent."

I want to urge you, therefore, to press on. There is no limitation that can stop you from reaching your desired goal or destination. The spirit of courage is at work in every one of us, particularly to you reading this book right now. That is the same spirit that inspired you to purchase this book. There is a hunger in your heart to do more than you are currently doing.

All you need is to stir it up. The greatest obstacle of the human potential is the fear of the unknown, but if you make a decision right now to press on and say yes to your dreams, yes to your potentials, yes to your skills, yes to your abilities, you will become unstoppable. Soon you will begin to unlock all other doors that has been limiting you from fulfilling your God-given potentials, and then the progress will begin and nothing can stop you.

Key Important Points to Note from the Foregoing Chapter

1. It makes no difference how many times you have been rejected or denied; if you persist in courage, you will eventually get the approval you need.
2. Most times in life, it will look as if the whole world is coming against you and everything you believe in seems to be falling apart. At such times, you need to stand your grand and press on with boldness toward your dreams because

if you don't give up, life will combine every event and circumstances for your good.
3. Make a courageous decision to never give up on your dreams no matter what life hands you. Success is just one step away, persist until you win.
4. Never allow someone else's opinion of you become your reality because you have hidden treasures of greatness within you; you are well equipped for the challenges that lies ahead.

Principle Four

Understanding the Purpose of Life

For everything, absolutely everything, above and below, visible and invisible, everything got started in him and find its purpose in him.
—Colossians 1:16 MSG

Some of the greatest discoveries emanating from my curiosity to discover the meaning and the essence of the human creature is that man is a spirit and that there are spiritual laws and precepts including promises that has been established from time immemorial by the supreme being, God, to help man navigate through life successfully. Without a conscious and careful adherence to this laws, the search for the meaning of life cannot be realized.

It is of utmost importance to understand that you cannot start living beyond your limitation until you understand the essence and meaning of your life. In other words beyond physical laws, natural laws, religious laws, etc. there are supernatural laws that supersedes all other laws. The potion that we read above in Colossians 1:16 categorically stated that everything, absolutely everything, started in him and find its purpose in him.

The day I came across this portion of the Bible, my life took on a new shape of understanding, and the more I comprehend this verse, the more I realized that my life is meaningless without a true encounter and relationship with God and his son, lord Jesus Christ. A British atheist, Bertrand Russell, made a profound statement when he said, "Unless you assume a God, the question of life purpose is meaningless."

What this means, therefore, is that the purpose of your life cannot be discovered in any other source away from the original source which is God, the supreme being and the creator of the whole universe; hence a lot of folks go about in ignorance, searching to understand the meaning and purpose of their lives in the wrong sources, which often end up in regrets, and until there is a shift in thought pattern and belief system, they will still be running around in a vicious circle, all to no avail.

I understand the effectiveness of the principles of determination, courage, persistence, self-confidence, and attitude, etc. in our day-to-day pursuit of goals and objective and toward realizing the purpose of our life; however, while all these qualities are required in accomplishing our purpose in life, I want to submit to you that there is more to life than just following these principles.

In the unfolding pages of this chapter, we will be understanding the true steps and precepts that will ultimately lead us to the realization of the true meaning and purpose of our life and how to begin applying them immediately into our own life. The search for the purpose of life has puzzled many philosophers for thousands of years.

The Bible recorded in the Book of Jeremiah 17:7–8 NLT stated, "Blessed are those who trust in the Lord and have made the Lord their hope and confidence. They are like trees planted in the riverbank, with roots that reach deep in to the water. Such trees are not bothered by the heat or worried by long months of drought. Their leaves stay green, and they never stop producing fruit."

The above verse we just read explained some of the wonderful promises that we can derive from trusting God, the supreme being and the creator of the universe. Oftentimes we go through life, struggling and languishing in ignorance because we fail to acknowledge God in our day-to-day decision undertakings. This also confirms what is recorded in the Book of Hosea 4:6, "My people are destroyed for lack of knowledge." Noticed that he did not say lack of money.

A lot of people that I interact with on daily basis are often quick to point out that not having enough money is the major reason why they have not been able to reach their goals in life. Some will complain to me how badly their past experiences, location they live in, family background, etc. has limited their progress, but I what to submit to you that your prosperity and progress will dramatically take a new turn the day you discover your purpose on earth, until you begin to give satisfactory answers to questions like, who am I, why am I here, why am I born at particular time like this, what is really the purpose of my life, what I am called to accomplish on this earth, etc. Hence in giving answers to these questions, we must have a necessity to understand that it all begins with God.

Thomas Carlyle made a profound statement when he said, "The man without a purpose is like a ship without a rudder—a waif, a nothing, a no man." In other words, the day you understand the purpose of your life, your life will take on a new meaning.

My own personal encounter with the Lord has brought meaning and purpose to my life, and this experience will continue to shape my everyday decisions for the rest of my stay on this earth. His extravagant grace and guidance has caused me to prosper and succeed beyond my wildest imagination. That is why I'm committed to making sure that the remaining pages of this chapter will be dedicated to showing you a step-by-step approach on how you, too, can discover your purpose through an encounter with him, the maker of the whole universe.

And it's so interesting to know that he is interested to start a relationship with you right now, right there where you are, not minding your past or present situation. He confirmed this in the Book of James 4:8, and it said, "Draw near to God, and he will draw near to you. Cleanse your hands, you sinners, and purify your hearts, you double-minded." It's of utmost importance to understand that the greatest tragedy of life is not death but living a life without purpose.

There is no other way that we can discover our purpose unless through a conscious relationship with our creator. Consider a new mobile phone you purchased from the store which is specially designed for mobile communication. Let's imagine you have never seen or used one before. You will not know how to operate and utilize the features that has been stored in the phone by the manufactural.

You might, therefore, need to study the manual script or visit the manufactural for direction on how to operate the mobile phone, but if you think otherwise and choose to use your own thinking to operate the phone, you might end up damaging some important features that are stored in the phone.

In other words, to effectively understand the usage or purpose of gadget or product, you need to seek direction from the maker or original source of the thing. Hence this analogy is applicable in our quest toward understanding the purpose of human life. In other words, the first step toward understanding the purpose of the human life will definitely be to refer back to the original source, which is God. The Bible confirmed this in the Book of Acts 17:28, "For in him we live and move and have our being. As some of your own poets have said, 'We are his offspring.'"

From the foregoing portion we read above, we can understand that we cannot do or accomplish anything on our own unless we begin to develop a consistence relationship with him, God. It is of utmost importance, therefore, to understand that we are created in God's image for a relationship with him; being in that relationship therefore is the only thing that can define the meaning and purpose of our life.

Jesus Christ said, "I am the bread of life. Whoever comes to me will never go hungry, and whoever believes in me will never be thirsty." Our greatest desire, therefore, should be to know God for that is the only true way we can discover the purpose and meaning of our life. We must continue to build and develop our relationship with him for that remain the sure part to realizing the true meaning of life, for without clear purpose life becomes boring and uninteresting.

Hence the first step toward establishing this very important relationship was recorded in the Book of Romans 10:9, "If you confess with your mouth 'Jesus is Lord' and believe in your heart that God raised him from the dead, you will be saved." In other words, accepting our Lord Jesus Christ simply means believing that he is the son of God. Note, we accept Jesus by faith, not through our works.

The Bible said, "God saves you by his extravagant grace through faith. When you believe, it is a gift from God, not your own doing."

Hence salvation is not given to you because of the good works you have done, so none of us can boast about it. This was made possible by his blood that was shared on the cross of Calvary for the remission of our sins.

Let's look at Isaiah 53:4, "Surely he took up our pain and bore our suffering, yet we considered him punished by God, stricken by him, and afflicted." In other words, the whole work of our salvation was settled in the cross of Calvary. The Bible said, "For God so loved the world that he gave his only begotten son that who so ever believeth in him should not perish but have everlasting life."

So all we have do to partake in these great promises are to believe and confess his lordship over our life. This is so important, for without God, life has no purpose, and without purpose, life has no meaning. And without meaning, life has no significance or hope. In the Bible, many people expressed this hopelessness; Isaiah complained, "I have labored in vain, I have spent my strength in vain and for nothing."

Another person that experienced this sense of hopelessness was Job. Job said, "My life drags by—day after hopeless day, and I give up. I am tired of living. Leave me alone. My live makes no sense." Hence from their lamentation, we can deduce that living a life without hope is the greatest tragedy that can happen to man, not death. But I have good news for you. I mean you that is reading this book right now.

If there is any time in your life that you have felt hopeless, hold on, wonderful changes are coming your way as you begin to align your life with the purpose he has established for you even before you were conceived in your mother's womb. He said, "I have good plans for you, not plans to hurt you. I will give you hope and a good future."

Friend, it makes no difference what kind of limitation that may be facing you right now, the grace of God is going to cause everything around you to begin to function for your good. And I pray that the knowledge and power of God will be revealed to you so that you can fully be enlightened about the purpose and meaning that he has for your life

Key Important Points to Note from the Foregoing Chapter

1. My purpose in life can only be realized through a constant and continues relationship with the supreme being, God.
2. The greatest tragedy of the human life is not death but living a life without purpose.
3. The major purpose of my life is to bring glory to my Creator through following his lay-down principles for my life.
4. Understanding my purpose and the meaning of my life helps clarify my everyday decision undertakings and priorities.

Principle Five

The Law of Preparation

Proper preparation prevents poor performance (PPPPP).
—Charlie Batch

Preparation is one of the most fundamental ingredients of success. Whatever project or task you have in your heart to accomplish must first begin with the questions of how, what, where, who, where, when, etc. Hence a thorough consideration must be given to each and every one of these questions for you to effectively navigate your way through the whole process of accomplishing your goals.

Your destiny is very much up to you; your future is largely determined by your everyday actions and decisions. Simply put, therefore, what you have achieve so far in your life is a result of your previous decisions and actions, and what you will achieve in the years to come will be dependent on your choices and actions today. Your future is in your own hands, if it's going to be, it's up to you.

In other words, there must be a plan and a strategy on how to maximize the ideas and resources available to you right now for a worthwhile accomplishment tomorrow. Everyone wants to be prosperous, happy, successful, and popular, but the only way to realize all this objective is to create it through hard work and good planning. You cannot afford to live your life by chance, hoping and believing that one day you will make it. Hope is not a strategy for success, you have to make a decision to create your own future because nothing will move until you make the first move. The majority of people tend to be passive in their responses and actions to life, they are constantly wishing and hoping that something good will happen to them.

You have to get out of that slow lane and start creating and working on your dreams and God-given potentials. It was Thomas Edison that said, "If we did all the things we are capable of, we would literally astound ourselves." An engineer who draws up a building plan knows that the height of the building will mostly be determined by how deep or strong the foundation of the building will be, that is the stronger or deeper the foundation of the building, the taller the building will be. This analogy is also true about success and failure in our own personal lives.

The more time and effort you put in to prepare for whatever thing you want to achieve in life, the more success and reward you will eventually accomplish in that area. In other words, all worthwhile accomplishments are products of proper and thoughtful preparation.

Hence the world needs men and women who are properly prepared academically, mentally, psychologically, physically, politically, and spiritually to successfully thrive in our fast-paced competitive generation. Most of the challenges we are facing in our political system, for example, can be linked to some of the poor choices we have made over the years.

Mostly when it comes to choosing who will pilot the affairs of our government, this poor choices has led to us instituting men and women in the arm of authority who are not fully prepared, mentally and professionally, to pilot the affairs of the state effectively which has resulted to the so many economic challenges that are affecting many nations around the world today. The importance of preparation in our day-to-day pursuit of our set goals and objectives cannot be overemphasize.

Most of the best accomplishment that has been recorded by great sports personalities in our generation today has more to do with preparation than skills and talent. Cristiano Ronaldo, the best soccer player in the world today, was asked by a super sports analyst how he has manage to maintain the top goal scoring record in the Spanish league for the past three years ruining. His response was practice,

practice, practice. He said that he practice seven days each week, working on perfecting and improving his goal-scoring skills.

The analyst asked him a second question, "But why do you still need to practice since you are already the best in the world?"

His response was, "Being the best in the world for me is one of the easiest status any achiever can attain in any field of life, but maintaining your position at the top will require constant and continues practice and improvement. That's why I am always working on improving my goal-scoring skills. Notwithstanding the fact that I'm the best in the world, I still work and prepare for the games that lies ahead."

The sports analyst asked again, "In conclusion, how many hours does it take you to prepare for a ninety-minute soccer game?"

His response, "I often start my preparation seven hours ahead of each game."

Did you notice that it takes him more time and effort to prepare for a game than the game itself? Now that is what I'm talking about. Preparation, therefore, can be said to be the pacesetter to all worthwhile accomplishment in life.

Great achievers always place preparation ahead of any other activity or success principle we might think of. They are never complaisant in anything they do, they are always working on mastering their craft. Hence from the foregoing interaction between Ronaldo and the sports analyst, we can categorically justify our assertion that success has more to do with hard work and personal effort than talent or skills.

In other words, a decision to constantly and continuously work on your abilities and giftings is one of the sure ways to remain at the top in whatever field of life you may find yourself. Your level of preparation is what will give you the competitive age among your competitors in any area of life. Here is my point, if you want to be the best in your class, invest more hours in your studies and class work, that is instead of two hours, increase your study hours to five hours or even eight hours. The more input you make, the greater your output. If you want to be the best as a salesman, invest more time in mastering the skills and psychology of selling.

In whatever field you are, you can get to the top only if you will constantly and continuously work on yourself and mastering the winning strategy. H. Jackson Brown Jr. confirmed this when he said, "The best preparation for tomorrow is doing your best today." This is why I always disagree with some of my friends when they make certain statement like, he is lucky to have gotten that promotion or she is lucky to have received that award, because for me there is no such thing as luck, success, promotion, or the attainment of anything worthwhile in life; it's a result of preparation meeting with opportunity. It was George Washington that said, "It is better to be prepared for an opportunity and have none than to have an opportunity and not be prepared."

In other words, before anything else, preparation is the key to success to succeed in anything in life. You must apply the principles of self-discipline and preparation to make any significant advancement; hence the higher the level of your preparation, the higher your success. Jack Canfield made a profound statement when he said, "I believe that people make their own luck by great preparation and good strategy."

In other words, to increase your chances of succeeding more in life, you have to increase the quality of your preparation. Jimmy Smits, a world boxing champion, was once asked, "Hey, Jimmy, what is the strategy that has made you stand out over the years in your career?" In response he said, "It's less about the physical training, in the end, than it is about the mental preparation. Boxing is a chess game. You have to be skilled enough and have trained hard enough to know how many different ways you can counterattack in any situation in any moment."

Once again the above response by Jimmy Smits confirms the efficacy of preparation in attaining anything worthwhile in life. Be it mental, physical, or psychological, preparation in any aspect of life remain the springboard of all worthwhile accomplishment.

Do you want to see excellence in your business, career, job, academics, or any area of life that you are interested in? Then you have to make a commitment to the law of preparation to be able to lead excellently in any area of specialization. You must make conscious deliberate commitment to properly prepare yourself, in that particular area of endeavor, by understanding the basis through personal effort and self-discipline.

Now here is my point, you can do anything you want to do, you can be anything you want to be, you can go anywhere you want to go if only you can properly prepare yourself through learning and discovering the essential factors that matters most in that particular area of life that you are interested in. Hence it is of utmost importance to understand that the beginning of any worthwhile project is always difficult. Let's take for example cultivating a farmland for plantation. You have to go all through the process of clearing the trees, grasses, and weeds in the farmland. Then again you have to till and cultivate the land to be able to finally plant your seeds and crops.

Note all those activities where the necessary preparatory stage must be undertaken to enable the successful growth of the crops, but if by whatever reason you choose not to follow those steps, you will not be able to achieve your ultimate goal of growing your crops effectively. Hence this analogy is also applicable in our own personal life goals and dreams. You must not take the preparatory stage of your dreams for granted because the better your preparation for the thing you want to achieve, the better and more effective your outcome result will be. It was the author and speaker Anthony Robins that said, "Success is processional."

In other words, success is taking one step at time. An old English proverb reads, "A journey of a thousand miles begins with a step." Anybody who is at the second floor of a building was once at the first floor; the only difference between him and another individual who is at the first floor is time and personal effort to make a move. One of the most important lessons I have learn in life is that you can literally change your life and become anything you want to be by making a daily commitment to work and develop yourself. It all boils down to a decision to patiently follow the process of preparation, self-discipline, and a vision of what you want to achieve to get there.

From the various analogies above, we can deduce that the term success is a component that is broken into different processes and stages. In other words, you cannot thrive or navigate properly in life by trying to overlook any stage that has been discussed so far in this book. Most importantly the preparatory stage, hence this stage, can also be likening to a soldier who is preparing for a war; in the case of a soldier, however, he needs to consistently brainstorm himself with positive self-talk—for example, I am strong enough, I'm capable enough, I can do it, I will overcome again. He needs to make an everyday commitment to training, learning new skills/tactics and strategy on how to overcome the task and challenges that lies ahead.

Also in life, the preparation stage calls for gaining experience, skills, and knowledge that is required to face the challenges that lies ahead. Friend, at this point I will like to submit to you that life is like a war. In other words, the more determined and prepared you are, the higher and further you will go in your field of interest. On your way to attaining greatness, you must have to develop what I call "mental toughness." This is the mentality that will keep you going even when everyone says no to you, even when no one believes or give you the support that you need to go to the next level of your career.

At this point you have to stick your foot on the ground and keep pushing, it makes no difference what your dreams and goals for the future may be. What I want you to understand, however, is that you can accomplish anything you have set out in your heart to achieve if only you can patiently prepare well for it. Preparation ahead of any task gives you the capacity and knowledge to overcome. Whenever you come across people who have taken time to prepare, be it in leadership, academics, acting, public speaking, etc., they are always distinguished among the crowd.

The Bible recorded a profound statement on the concept of preparation in the Book of Proverbs 22:29 KJV, "Seest thou a man diligent in his business? He shall stand before kings; he shall not stand before mean men."

The term diligent as used above can also be rephrased as skilled or expert. In other words, it takes a consistence development of your skills through personal development to achieve excellence in life; hence many people in business today think that they can start at the top and work up. They are in a hurry, so they pay less concern to mastering the basics of their jobs. They fail to understand that long-term success is a result of becoming skilled and excellent at what you do.

In conclusion, therefore, I want you to understand that anything worthwhile takes a long time to accomplish. I challenge you, therefore, to patiently prepare yourself for the challenges that lies ahead by constantly working on your skills and abilities. There are thousands of individuals who have started from difficult backgrounds with little or no financial resources but have risen to the top of their careers through hard work and good planning, and if they can do it, you too can do it. Say yes to your dreams, say yes to your unfolding future, it's possible.

Key Important Points to Note from the Foregoing Chapter

1. Whatever you want to accomplish in life is possible through personal effort and good planning strategy.
2. Make a commitment to constantly and continually develop yourself in any area of interest that you have decided to follow to achieve your dreams. And be the best at it.
3. Above all understand that your future is in your own hands, only you can bring your dreams to reality; if it's ever going to happen, it's up to you.
4. At the beginning of any project or endeavor, always seek to understand the basic questions of how, what, who, when, and where. A thorough understanding of these questions, therefore, is the springboard of all worthwhile success.

Principle Six

Change Your Perception

> What is the difference between an obstacle and
> an opportunity? Our attitude toward it.
> —J. Sidlow Baxter

Life is all about perception. The way you perceive and approach issues and events whether positive or negative will affect the results you will ultimately produce. The term perception has been defined in psychology as the process by which people translate sensory impressions into a coherent and a unified view of the world through often unverified and unreliable information.

Hence from the above definition, we can deduce that our perception plays a critical role on our everyday decision-making. In other words, our perception determines how we react to the events and things that happens around us on daily basis. They, therefore, guide our behavior, attitudes, and approach toward life. What this means is that the outcome you will eventually get from challenges that are facing you right now will largely be determined by your perception toward them. Each time you are faced with a challenge, do you see the opportunity that lies in the other side of the challenge, or do just concentrate on the risk and problems that are created by your imaginations?

I want you to understand that all worthwhile accomplishment is largely influenced by your thoughts and perception toward them.

We may not have the power to completely change the events of our lives, but I do believe we have the power to change our perception toward them. Here is my point, the more you perceive and act positively toward your dreams, the more success you will eventually accomplish and vice versa.

In other words, until your perception and approach toward life changes, your life will not change. For things to change, you have to change the way you perceive and evaluate the circumstances and events in your life because poor evaluation leads to a poor life. Positive and creative evaluation leads to a rich and progressive life. By altering your perception and evaluation about events that are currently going on in your life, you can literally transform the world around you.

It was Dr. Wayne Dyer that said, "If you change the way you look at things, the things you look at change." In the same vain, give a gun to a soldier. He will use it to protect and fight for the peace of his country; give same weapon to an armed robber, he will use it to burgle your house and take away your valuables. It all boils down to the way the weapon was perceived by these two different individuals. Our perception, therefore, guides our everyday reactions to the circumstances of our lives and ultimately determines how successfully we can navigate through the circumstances and challenges of our contemporary world.

I want to submit to you that you can literally transform the circumstances and events of your life by changing your perception and evaluation toward them. The way you view or perceive a challenge in your life will affect your attitude and approach toward it, even before you make an effort toward solving it.

In other words, the difference between an obstacle and an opportunity are our perception toward them. Let me give you an example of the point I'm trying to prove. A shoe industry in the United States sent two of their salesmen to a remote country in Africa to create a new market for their products in order to increase their business reach. The first salesman that arrived in the city got frustrated within the first three days he spent in the city and reported back to his industry management that shoe manufacturing business will not thrive in this part of the world because he discovered that people living over there don't wear shoes. His company felt disappointed and withdrew him from the trip and sent the second salesman.

The second salesman stayed in the city for two days and reported with a different observation from the previous salesman. In his words, he said, "What a big marketing opportunity we have in this part of the world. I discovered that people don't wear shoes in this part of the world. All we need to do is to teach them the importance and beauty of wearing shoes. And we don't have competitors down here. I believe in a process of time, we'll start making a fortune of income here."

Did you observe the important difference between these two salesmen? While the first salesman was focusing his observation on the challenges, the second salesman, however, focused his own observation on the opportunities that are within the challenges. This illustration confirms the words of Apostle Yiga Francis when he said, "Many look but only few see." An artist can be very rude if you disturb him before he accomplishes what he is intending to design because he perceives and sees differently from those who are not artist. He may stop by your house and beg you for a stone and maybe you have walked passed that stone several times without noticing the potential beauty that might come out from that stone. The dogs might have been doing stuff on it, but the artist walked into your yard and saw something beautiful in that stone, beyond what you can imagine. Two months later when the artist invites you to his workshop, he says to you, "Do you see that art? Do know where it came from?" Your response maybe "England or France." "No," says the artist, "it came from your house." You said, "Really, how much is it?" He said, "Five hundred dollars, please."

So you see, all these years you had $500 lying dormant in your yard, but you couldn't recognize it because of your perception of what you thought it was. But the artist came and saw the potential and turned it in to a fortune. The fundamental lesson from the story means that by changing your perception and evaluation of things and events around you, you can literally transform your life.

In other words, it's not what happen to you that count, it's the way you interpret and evaluate what happen to you that will make all the difference. For things to change, you have to change your thought and perception about certain things in your life. It is important, therefore, to realize that there is something special about your life. Don't let anyone tell you what you can do or cannot do. Don't let their interpretation of you become your reality. You have something special, you have a gift, your life has a meaning, but you must learn to perceive and act accordingly to be able to unleash your true potential. I may not know anything about your life, but I'm so certain that you have something priceless to offer to our world.

The only thing that can really stop you from achieving your goals is you, your perception about things around you. Hence the moment you begin to look at every challenge in your life with a positive mind-set, the progress will begin.

It was Jim Britt who said, "For things to change, you have to change. For things to get better, you have to get better." Here is the fact, nothing is ever going to change in your life until you decide to change. You have to change your belief system, priority, perception, and this will conversely change the way you approach the issues of life. Therefore, change is something you must accept if you are ready to move forward.

American famous philosopher Zig Ziglar confirmed this when he said, "Until your mentality changes, your life will not change." A positive mental attitude is the starting point of all riches and major progress in our world. I commend you, therefore, to start renewing your mind with positive thoughts. Thoughts like, it is possible, I can make it happen, I will overcome, and this too will pass, etc. Again surround yourself with the right kind of friends and stay away from negative people.

The kind of friends you hang around with will play a major role on your perception and interpretation of things around you. The fact is that whoever will not increase you, will eventually decrease you. In other words, one of the most important decisions you must make for things to change in your life is changing your friends. It is impossible to hang around negative people all the time and make progress. An English adage says, "Show me your friend and I will tell you who you are."

Author and writer Charles "Tremendous" Jones confirmed this when he said, "There are two things that will determine how far you will go in life, the kind of friends you have and the kind of books you read." Let me give a short story. Two partners go bankrupt in their various business. One partner jumped out of the window of a ten-story building and die. The other partner goes on a monthlong vacation to refresh and reorganize his life; he comes back with a new strategy and started his business all over again and becomes very successful within a short period of time. This is a true life story. They both experience the same circumstances but choose to interpret it differently.

The lesson remains the same. It is not what happens to you, it is how you perceive and evaluate what happens to you that will make the difference in your life. Your success, prosperity, and failure are all products of your thoughts and perception about things and events around you. In other words, change your perception, and your life will follow suit. Reality does not bite, it's our perception of reality that bite.

Key Important Points to Note from the Foregoing Chapter

1. Our success and failure in any area of your life is largely dependent on how you perceive and evaluate issues in that area.
2. The way you view or perceive a challenge in your life will affect your approach toward solving it, or things to change in your life. You have to develop the attitude of looking at every challenge in your life with a possibility and a positive mind-set. Believe that it is possible.
3. Understand that it makes no difference of the level of challenge that is facing you right now. Rather it's your interpretation of the challenge that will determine whether you will triumph or fail.

Principle Seven

Change Your Priority

One very important fact I have discovered in life is that people can literally change their lives by changing their priorities.
—Kennedy King

Previously in chapter 6, we have been able to establish the various ways that our perception of things and events around us affects our decisions on daily basis; hence the same way, our perception influences the results of our lives. Our daily priorities affect us even more.

The term priority can literally be defined as what an individual value most in his or her life, what means more to him or her, what he can really spend majority of his time doing. The *Oxford Advanced Learner's Dictionary* defines the term priority as that particular thing in an individual's life that means more or that is perceived to be more important than any other thing and should be dealt with first before any other thing.

The question now is what you consider to be the most important thing in your own life right now? Whatever it may be, the moment you focus all your time and ability on it, you will begin to actualize the benefits and results that you so desire to actualize out of that thing.

In other words, the only thing limiting you from accomplishing that dream or target you have set for yourself is because you have not made it a top priority in your life. The moment you begin to set your priorities straight, the progress will begin. If it is important to you, you will find a way, if it is not, you will find an excuse. It all boils down to what you value most in your life at a particular time.

Let's say for example if you want to be rich. It is possible. But you have to open up your mind to understanding the principles and laws of money; so it goes for happiness, relationships, and whatever thing you want to accomplish in life. The moment you make anything in your life a priority, the possibilities and ideas on how to attain them will begin to manifest. It's as simple as that. In other words, by changing your priorities, you can literally transform your entire life. Your priorities and choices today will eventually determine your level of accomplishment tomorrow.

Here is my point, by hanging around the right kind of friends, reading the right kind of books, and putting God first in whatever you do today, you are automatically setting up yourself for a greater outcome tomorrow. The fact is that your everyday choices will ultimately determine your future. In other words, making the right choices today will definitely determine the level of your success tomorrow and vice versa. It all depends on you. If you are ever going to amount to anything worthwhile in life, it will largely be depended on your ability to put first things first in your life.

Here is my point, the day your priorities change, your life will take on a new positive meaning. Remember it's not about speed, it's about direction. I want to submit to you that until you begin to make some critical decisions about your life and get some of your major priorities straight, you will keep running around like someone in a vicious circle, without any tangible result to show.

The fact is that any successful person you see today was not born with riches or his accomplishments. Rather it was as a result of setting the right priorities and taking the right steps that brought him or her the accomplishments.

For things to change, you must begin to ask yourself the right kind of questions:

1. What is the most important thing in my life right now?
2. What do I really value most in life?

3. What do I spend most of my time doing on daily basis?
4. Where and who do I spend most of my time with?

Hence a conscious evaluation and right answers to the above questions will redirect the affairs of your life to a new and more productive adventure. Let us take a critical look again at the first question. What is the most important thing in my live right now?

The inability to answer this question correctly is one of the major problems of our young people today because the moment a man can understand especially what the most important thing that he needs to focus on, the way to accomplish it, becomes shorter and even clearer. In other words, the knowledge of what you want out of life is like a road map that is guiding you to your actual destination. A lot of folks go about life aimlessly, not knowing what they really want out of life, that is what you may call it a misplaced priority.

Whenever you come across such people, they are always unstable in what they do. They spend their precious time on things that are less important to their own progress. If you are reading this book and you seriously desire a change in your life, you can only realize it by thoughtfully pinpointing what is the most important aspect of your life that requires more time and attention. The moment you understand it and consciously work on that area, your life will begin to take on a more productive and meaningful existence. Be it your academics, business, relationship, or financial, destiny, whatever area of your life it may be. The moment you make a decision to focus on that area, a corresponding change and advancement will be activated in that area of your life. And the progress will begin. Another question you must critically examine if you truly desire a change in your live is the question, "Where and who do I spend most of my time with on a daily basis?"

It was Charles "Tremendous" Jones that said, "What you will become in five years from now will be determined by what you read and who you associate with." In other words, your close associates will either make you all or mar you. You must surround yourself with friends that can uplift and instill in you. The right mind-set to succeed is again to pay close attention to where you spend most of your time.

The environment and location you live in also play a major role in building up your mind-set and personality. If the environment you are living is not upgrading you, it will eventually degrade and relegate you to the background.

Hence here is my point, for things to change, you have to change your friends, change your environment, and ultimately change your everyday choices and priorities. You have to understand that who you are today is a result of the choices you made yesterday. And your tomorrow will largely be dependent on the choices you are making today. Your future, therefore, is in your own hands. If it's ever going to be, it's up to you. Never let the opinions of others stop you from reaching out to your great potentials. Understand the fact that not everyone will like or support you. But you have to believe and have confidence in your abilities and the possibilities that lies ahead for you. Understand also that only you can bring your dreams to reality. No one else will.

Therefore, on daily basis, you have to be conscious of your decisions because any decision you take from now onward is either going to make you or destroy you. Understand that the decision to change is one decision you must make, and only you can make it for yourself.

Many folks are afraid to change to new ways of doing things, afraid to change friends, afraid to learn new skills, or even go back to school because they are letting their comfort zone stop them from venturing into new horizons. The fact is that we all have twenty-four hours in a day, what then is the difference between the poor and the rich? It is the quality that is inputted in to the time that makes the difference.

Hence while the rich allot more quality time to the things that matters most in his life and business, the poor waste his own precious time doing things that matters less to his life and business. It's that simple. However, the moment an individual gets his priorities straightened up, existence will definitely take on a new shape.

In other words, your decision to change your daily priorities today is your receipt for a greater outcome tomorrow. But the problem with many folks today is that they have become so comfortable with their old ways of doing things they don't want to try new things. They don't want to find out better ways of doing whatever they are doing. But the fact still remains that whatever you are doing right now, there are faster and more effective way of doing it. If only you can open up your mind to accepting new trends and advancement in our world today.

Here is my point, get yourself unstock from that old method and start opening your mind to learn things because times are changing. You also have to change so that you can compete favorably with the new trends of things. Learn new skills, go back to school, try new methods, make new friends, and ultimately change your mentality so that you can start achieving your best in your chosen field. And finally understand that until your daily priorities change, your life will never change and vice versa.

Key Important Points to Note from the Foregoing Chapter

1. For things to change, you have to change your daily priorities. In other words, spend more time on things that matters most in your life.
2. Our choices today, be it positive or negative, will determine the level of your accomplishment tomorrow.
3. You will be the same person you are today even in the next five years unless you change you close associates and the kind of books you read.
4. The moment you focus all your attention and ability on one particular area of your life, the result or progress you so desire in that area will begin to spring fort.

Principle Eight

Attitude Is Everything

> There is a very little difference in people. But that little difference makes a very big difference. The little difference is attitude. The big difference is whether it is positive or negative.
> —John C. Maxwell

Your attitude and approach to life is at the core of your personality. In other words, the totality of what you will achieve in life will largely be determined by your attitude. When you approach life with an optimistic and positive attitude, people will open doors of opportunity for you that would be close for many others.

If you truly want to experience more success and progress in your personal life, you owe it to yourself to develop the personality that radiates optimism and self-confidence in whatever thing you set your heart to accomplish. Your attitude has a lot to do with the level of success you can attain in life. Your attitude is like a magnet that attracts the right kind of circumstances and people your way.

I like the way William James puts it, "The greatest revolution of our generation is the discovery that human beings, by changing the inner attitude of your minds, can change the outer aspects of their lives." Your attitude reflects your inner conversation whether positive or negative through your actions, and your actions in the other hand determines how people perceives and responds to you in any given situation. In other words, developing a positive and optimistic attitude at the beginning of every life venture is a necessary ingredient for your long-term success.

Here is my point, we can set goals, make plans, and even pray. But without the right mental attitude, our success will be limited. You need to wake up every day with a mind-set of possibilities, with a sense of confidence and belief in yourself. Feed your mind with thoughts like, I'm smart enough, I'm the best, I will overcome, I can make it happen, I am capable enough, I have what it takes, this too will pass. When you continually talk to your self this way, your mind will begin to expand to the possibilities of the dreams and targets you have set for your life and career, and nothing will be impossible to you. Before long you will develop a winning attitude and begin to attract the right kind of friends and partnership that will take you to the next level of your career.

If you consistently maintain a positive attitude and consistently work to do your best in any situation, eventually you will overcome your immediate limitations and open up new opportunities for advancement in your personal life and career. You may not be able to control the events and circumstances of your life, but you can always control your attitude and response toward them. There are plenty of things in life that we have no control over. For example, there is absolutely nothing we can do about how people react to us or our products and services. All we can do, however, is to control the way in which we respond. Yet oftentimes we let the reactions and opinions of others dictate our outlook to life.

Here is my question, how do you react to failure or a little setback in your life? Do walk away discouraged and complain about it to everyone, or do you take control and stay focused? Accept the lessons learned. and move on with your life. Understand that success is 10 percent what happened to you and 90 percent how you judge and react to what happened to you.

Hence the way you react and respond to any given situation reflects your attitude. In other words, what you think, what you say, what you believe about your self are all within your control and are ultimately displayed by your attitude. You must first understand that your attitude is 100 percent under your control. And then learn to take charge of it at all times, notwithstanding the situation. You must address these issues and take on a new positive and optimistic view of the world for you to move forward.

American author and speaker Zig Ziglar made a profound statement when he said, "Your future depends on many things but mostly on you." In other words, to truly succeed in any endeavor in life, you have to first of all believe in your own abilities even if no one believes in you or give you the support that you require. You have to go for what you want with a mind-set of courage and possibilities because if you can see beyond your limitations, you will eventually begin to live beyond them. There is literally no obstacle that can stop the will of a man with a positive attitude. It makes no difference who likes you or supports you; the most important thing is the belief and thoughts you have about yourself. The only opinion that counts is the opinion you have about yourself. The Bible teaches us in the Book of Proverbs 4:23, "Keep your heart with all diligence for out of it spring the issues of life."

The fact is that you are the prophet of your own life. You have the power to attract to yourself whatever thing that you desire through the thoughts and convictions that dominate your mind on daily basis.

In other words, don't let the negative views of others about you stop you from going after your dreams. Take complete control of your thoughts and response to every challenge that life throws at you. Never interpret an obstacle, discomfort, pain, or failure as proof not to venture into your dreams or to quit, going after the targets that you have set for yourself. You owe it to yourself to make your dreams come true. Nobody is going to do it for you. It's your dream; even if no one is seeing it, you have to see it for yourself and believe in it. Wake up every day with a mind-set that you are blessed and highly favored by the most high God. And that nothing can stop you from living your dreams.

This is the exact attitude that has brought me where I am today. And if it worked for me, it will do the same for you too. One of the greatest discoveries of my life is that if an individual consistently and persistently pursue his dreams and desires with faith, courage, and determination, the universe will begin to attract circumstances, resources, and human connections that will work for his favor. In other words, there is nothing you cannot accomplish if you decide today to go after them with the right mind-set and attitude.

Let me give you a little story about my experience. When I was trying to get into college, I actually grew up from a poor background in Africa, and back in those days, we experienced a lot of challenges. Paying my way through high school was hard. And sometimes we struggled to complete a two square meals a day, things where really rough for us. My dad was a petty trader living in a foreign country. But on one occasion, he got in to trouble with the immigration department of the country that he was living in. The government has made controversial immigration policy at the time which adversely affected his stay in the country. And as a result, he was thrown inside the prison for five years.

That experience brought more hardship to our family because it affected his business, and no money was coming from his own side to support the family while I and my siblings where living in my country, Nigeria, with my mom who was managing a small business to take care of me my sister and three brothers.

It was hard for her to take care of the family alone with her small business. Those were really tough times for me and my siblings, but I looked at all those limitations and said to myself that I will live my dreams, not minding my family background or present conditions. I went on and told my mama about my interest in writing the upcoming college entry exams. And she said to me, "You know our family income at the moment, and you know that nobody in our family has ever been to the college before. Where are you going to get the money that will get you through the process?"

I said, "I don't know how, but I'm going to register for the exams from the little money I have saved up from the side job I was doing." So I stepped out in faith and wrote the exams, and to the glory of God, I scored through. That success brought about a chain reaction, and doors began to open for me, support began to spring fort from strangers, people who saw my dreams and believed in it. I choose to call them destiny helpers. I went through college and graduated successfully, and the rest was history. Today I hold a bachelor's degree in philosophy and currently pursuing a master's program in health informatics.

I was living in America, one of the finest countries in the world. If I could overcome all those limitations and still live my dreams, I strongly believe it's possible for you too. Only if you can decide to step out in faith and courage. The secret was a belief and confidence in my abilities and a decision to succeed, not minding the prevailing conditions. I, therefore, challenge you to take total control of your mind.

It makes no difference what your current circumstances may look like or how many times you have failed. The moment you take control of your mind and dominant thoughts, your life will take on an entirely new meaning and purpose. The only thing that can really stop you from living your dreams is you. But when you decide to step out in faith and determination with a strong belief and confidence in yourself, nothing can stop you. Whatever your life dream may be, I want you to realize that it's going to take your ability to develop the right kind of attitude, drive, commitment, and faith to realize it.

Former president Thomas Jefferson remarked, "Nothing can stop the man with the right mental attitude from achieving his goal. Nothing on earth can help the man with the wrong mental attitude." In other words, it all boils down to your dominant thoughts. Hence when your attitude is positive and conducive to growth, the mind expands, and the progress begins. "There is very little difference in people, but that little difference makes a very big difference. That little difference is attitude, the big difference is whether it's positive or negative," as remarked by John C. Maxwell.

For example, when an individual with a negative attitude is confronted by a challenge, he tends to make self-limiting statements such as, I don't think I will ever get over this, it's not going to be possible, no one has overcome it in the past, I'm not capable enough, I don't have the connections, etc. All these and many more are what I call self-limiting thoughts. And if these thoughts are not reprogramed by self-uplifting thoughts like, I'm smart enough, I can make it happen, let's give it a try, it is possible, the individual will eventually be hindered by his own thoughts. Even without taking a chance to see what is possible for him or not. In other words, the question of whether you will succeed or not is a question that only you can answer. No else is going to answer it for you. It's totally up to you. I suggest you to reprogram your mind with self-uplifting thoughts as stated above.

Thomas Edison, one of the most prolific inventors in history, was regarded by his teachers as a hard learner back in his college days. But he refused to let their opinion and interpretation of his personality stop him from unleashing his God-given potentials. And today he is regarded as America's greatest inventor.

Here is my point, you have to decide that nothing will stop you from living your dreams. It makes no difference the thoughts and opinion of others concerning you.

Finally it's not your condition, location, or current circumstances that will determine how far you will go in life. Rather it's your attitude, decision, and approach toward life that will eventually make the big difference. Believe in yourself and go after whatever you want with optimism, there are no limits.

Key Important Points to Note from the Foregoing Chapter

1. There is literally nothing you cannot accomplish when your attitude and approach toward life are positive and optimistic.
2. Your success in life is 10 percent what happened to you and 90 percent your attitude and approach toward it.
3. By changing your self-limiting thoughts to self-uplifting thoughts, you can literally transform your life and take complete control of your mind.
4. Your life achievements will be dependent on many things but mostly on your attitude and response to life challenges. In other words, the more positive you are about what life throws at you, the more successful you will eventually become and vice versa.

Principle Nine

The Power of Determination

Nothing splendid has ever been achieved except by those who dared believe that something inside of them was superior to circumstance.
—Bruce Barton

One of the core principles of living beyond your limitations is the power of determination. This principle simply states that when you consistently and persistently go after whatever you want in life with courage and determination and with the help of God, you will eventually get the answers that you are seeking.

In other words, your ability to persist in the face of setbacks and life challenges is a fundamental determinant factor to the level of your accomplishment. Success is not an accident. Success is the definite result of continues, persistent action in the unrelenting pursuit of your goals. Once an individual is determined, there are really no limits to what he can accomplish. This is one quality that will separate you from everyone else.

In other words, the difference between the possible and the impossible lies in a man's determination. The question is, how determined are you to succeed? How badly do you want it? My guarantee is that if you want it badly enough to give it all your best with persistence and determination, nothing can stop you. However, the fact that you have read this book up to this point is a proof that you are determined to turn your dreams into reality.

All you need right now is to eliminate whatever fear or procrastination that has been holding you back from taking action because ultimately I believe that the main essence of education is not knowledge but action. In other words, your ability to act boldly on what you know is what will eventually determine the level of what you get done. The fact is that the power and potentials that lies within you are way stronger than the fears and perceived limitations that tends to dominate your imaginations. The moment that you have a clear view of what you really want to accomplish coupled with a determined mind-set, there are no limits to what you can accomplish.

In order to bring your penitential and dreams to limelight and stand out in your field of endeavor, you need a burning desire coupled with a hunger and a determined spirit for success, a spirit that never accepts no for an answer. Realize that.

Whatever thing you want to achieve in life, it's possible. But you have to develop a determination that is strong enough to withstand the storms that will be thrown your way by the challenges of life. It is of utmost importance to understand that life is not going to be rosy and easy. In other words, you need to develop the mental stamina backed up with passion and determination to navigate smoothly over the challenges that lies ahead.

Author and motivational speaker Les Brown told an inspiring story that reflects the spirit of determination and persistence. He narrated that him and his twin brother were adopted by Mamie Brown, a kitchen worker and maid at the Miami state sanitarium district shortly after their birth in a poverty-stricken Miami neighborhood.

During his high school days, Les was placed under a special education program because of his hyperactivity and slow process of assimilating academic information and was regarded as mentally retarded by his high school teachers throughout his high school years. He went on to become a sanitation worker in Miami beach. But his ultimate dream was to be a disc jockey. At night, he will take a transistor radio to bed where he listened to the local jive-taking deejays. He created an imaginary radio station in his tiny room with its torn vinyl flooring. He constructed a hairbrush that served as his microphone as he practiced his patter, introducing records to his ghost listeners. His mother and brother could hear him through the thin walls and would shout at him to quit flapping his jaws and go to sleep.

But Les never listened to them. He was wrapped up with an obsession and determination to leave his dream. Then one day, Les boldly went to a local radio station during his lunch break from mowing grass for the city. He got into the station manager's office and told him that he wanted to be a disc jockey.

The manager looked at him and inquired, "Young man, do you have any background or experience in broadcasting?"

"No, sir, I don't."

The manager replied, "Well, young man, we don't have any position for you then."

Les thank him politely and left. The manager assumed that he has seen the last of this young man. But he underestimated Les Brown's commitment to his dream. He showed up again the next day acting as if he is seeing the manager for the first time.

He greeted, "Good morning, Mr. Butterball, my name is Les Brown."

"Oh yes, I know what your name is," replied the manager.

"I like to know if there is any job available for me."

"Didn't I tell you yesterday that there is no job available for you."

"Yes, sir, you did, but I don't know if someone was laid off or got fired, sir."

He said, "No one was fired or laid off, now get out of here."

He left and came back the next day, with a smiling face acting as if he is seeing him for the first time. "Hello, Mr. Butterball, how are you, sir?"

He said, "Fine, what you want now?"

Les replied and said, "I like to know if you have any job."

"Didn't I tell you the last two days we don't have any jobs?"

He said, "Yes, sir, you did. But I don't know if anyone got sick or died, sir."

He said, "No one got sick or died, and now don't ever come here again." He closed his office and threw him out again.

Les was still passionate and determined about his dream to be a disc jockey. So he showed up again the next day, acting as if he is seeing the manager for the first time. He smiled and said, "Hello, Mr. Butterball, how you are doing today, sir?"

The manager looked at him with a smiling face and said, "Come on, go get me a cup of coffee."

And from that day onward, Les was given the opportunity to work with the radio station; his persistence and determination finally paid off. He, however, started as an errand boy going to pick up entertainers for interviews from the airport. He never had a driver's license. But he was acting as if he had one. So once in a while, Les will walk in to the office to watch and study how the media presenters practice and display their shows.

Doing that, he was studying and mastering how the presenters were performing their craft until one day when his opportunity finally came. One of the presenters couldn't finish his show because he was drunk. The manager noticed it and called on Les to cover him up but warned him not to say anything. However, Les was hungry and has been waiting patiently for such an opportunity to showcase his skills. He said in his mind now, *He is going to think I'm crazy.*

He went on and called his girlfriend, Casandra, and his mom; he told them to get ready and that he is about to come on air. Les moved in gently and sat down at the turntable. He was ready and hungry. He flipped on the microphone switch and said, "Look out this is me LB, triple P Les Brown, your platter playing poppa. There were none before me and there will be none after me. Therefore, that makes me the one and only. Lover and single, love to mingle. Certified, bona fide, indubitable qualified to bring you certification, a whole lot of action. Look out, baby, I'm your love man."

He was hungry. He gained the confidence of his manager and his audience from that fateful beginning. He went on to enjoy a successful career in broadcasting, politics, and motivational speaking. This story, as we can see, is a fundamental example of how far the quality of persistence and determination can take you in the pursuit of realizing your God-given potentials. The truth is that for you to really succeed in a fast-paced and competitive generation that we are facing today, you need to be determined.

The term determination as we said earlier is the quality that instigates an individual to consistently and continually try to do something even when it seems impossible until it is accomplished. This is one quality that draws the line between champions and failures. Individuals who are determined are not always understood. They are those kinds of people you can describe as no-limit people. They don't accept that something is impossible just because everybody accepts it. They are always willing to go the extra mile, they are always willing to push beyond limits, they don't let circumstances or the opinions of others stop them from going after the goals that they have set for themselves.

That's the kind of mentality that I think we should all develop if truly we want to turn our dreams to reality. Too many people give up too soon in life because they are unable to push beyond limit. Friend, you need to dig your heels in and say, "I know what I have on the inside. I am a child of God. I am full of his grace and wisdom. And that I am going to become all that he has created me to be."

Apostle Paul made a remarkable statement in the Bible. He said to Timothy, "Stir up the gift of God in you." We all have something special and precious about our lives the moment we realize that particular thing and act on it. Our entire life will begin to take on a whole different meaningful direction. So today I'm saying to you, stir up the gift, skills, ideas, and potentials, etc. that are lying dormant within you.

You have the gift of God upon your life. There is greatness within you, but you have to shake off the fear of failure and past experiences that has been stopping you from acting on your dreams. The Bible teaches that the gift of a man maketh way for him. Therefore, it's time to take action. I want to remind you that God wants to do a new thing in your life, not minding how negative and rough your past has been; he wants to give you a fresh start. Don't give up, don't go around thinking that your life has come to a dead end or maybe that you have reached your limits.

I know you may say, "Kennedy, you don't know me, you don't know my current situation, I have gone as far as my education can take me, I have exhausted all my possibilities." Yes, it's true I may not know you, but I do know our God and his abilities to transform your life if only you can hang in there with determination and call on him. I want you to get up every morning and put your head up and say to yourself, "I have come too far to give up now. I may be knocked down, but I am not knocked out." Declare aloud to yourself many times every day, "I am going to get back up again."

Keep pressing, keep believing that you were not made to be average, you were made to excel. Learn to start each day with words like, I am talented, I am creative, I am highly favored by God, I will see my dreams come to pass. Declare those words with faith, and before long you will begin to see them in reality. I want you to realize that throughout the journey of life, you are going to be encounter forces that will be trying to stop you from becoming all that God has created you to be. But you must continually remind yourself that you are well able and equipped by your heavenly Father to see your dreams come through.

Sometimes it may look as if your life is empty and noting much is going your way and anything you try to do seems impossible. At this time, you have to dig in your heels and continually remind yourself that you have a gift on the inside, that you are talented and well able to overcome your limitations. Decide today, once and for all, to take total control of your own life. Understand that what happened in your past is not nearly as important to what is in your future. Where you are going is much more important to where you have been. One thing is sure, if you stay focused on the past, you are likely to miss numerous excellent opportunities that lies ahead. And the fact is that no matter where you are in life, you can get better. It all starts from your thinking.

Never allow circumstances or people's opinion of you to convince you that you are never going to rise higher or that you will never see your dreams come through. Don't believe those lies, instead take courage and say to yourself; "I have a gift in the inside, my life will not end like this, I will leave to see my dreams come to past." Keep pressing forward and keep believing, keep yourself stirred up.

Don't allow your temporally limitations to keep you from seeing God's promises fulfilled in your life. And I want to advise you to stay away from energy drainers, I mean people who has nothing meaningful to contribute to your life. The Bible teaches us in the Book of Proverbs, "He who walketh with the wise shall be wise, but a companion of fools shall be destroyed."

A number of years ago, I found myself in a stagnation point in my life. I was unproductive and unable to see God's direction clearly. One day I noticed that almost all of my friends were in the same situation. So each time we got together, our problems were what we often talked about. As I prayed about it, God showed me that I needed some foundational-level people in my life. Such individuals that can bring out the best in my life. And that was a turning point in my own personal life. As I began to meet new people, my perspective and idea about life took a more meaningful direction; this is where the people who brought out the best in me. And after all these years, I have concluded that it's better to be alone than with the wrong company. Because it's so amazing how a single conversation with the right person can dramatically change and improve the perspective you have about yourself and the possibilities that lies ahead of you.

In other words, you must learn to remove yourself from negative thinking company. Finally I advise you to take a closer look at your associations because it is a fundamental indication of where your life is headed to. An old English adage says, "Show me your friend, and I will tell you who you are." It is therefore of utmost importance to understand that by changing who you associate with, you can literally change the direction of your life. Hence I encourage you to surround yourself with positive-minded people and finally make a courageous decision today that nothing will stop you from getting to the top of your career and that you will stay focused and determined until you see your expectations come to manifestation.

The Bible in the Book of Proverbs 23:18 gives us an assurance of a glorious future. It said, "Surely there is a future, and your hope shall not be cut off." In other words, if you stay focused and determined, you will see your dreams come true. I encourage you to keep pushing, you are closer than you can ever imagine. The next step you take could open up all the doors that you have been searching for. Never give up yourself because God has not given up on you.

Key Important Points to Note from the Foregoing Chapter

1. There is literally nothing you cannot accomplish once you have a clear view of what you want and the determination to go after it even in the means of difficulties and setbacks.
2. The difference between the possible and the impossible lies in a man's determination. In other words, there is nothing like it is impossible, it all depends on how baldly you want it.
3. If you persistently and consistently go after whatever you want in life, with the help of the supreme being, God, you will eventually accomplish your heart's desires.
4. Make it an attitude to always go the extra mile in whatever goal you have set for yourself because oftentimes we tend to give up to soon without realizing how close we are to our breakthrough.

Principle Ten

The Power of Decision

> It's not what we do once in a while that shapes
> our lives. It's what we do consistently.
> —Anthony Robbins

Wherever you see significant achievements in any aspect of life, someone must have been taking some courageous decisions to attain them. I personally believe that the difference between the poor and the rich in our society today lies on the quality of decisions each and every one of them make on a daily basis.

A lot of folks let the opinion and decisions of others determine what they do or what they should pursue in life instead of taking charge and controlling their own destiny. They entrust their future in the hands of others.

It was Bill Cosby that said, "I don't know the key to success, but the key to failure is trying to please everybody." In other words, you owe it to yourself to chart the course of your own life through your decisions and actions on a daily basis.

Only you can sing your own song, write your own book, make your own invention, create your own art, etc. Your destiny is completely in your hands, don't let anyone tells you what you can do or what you cannot do. Take responsibility of your own life because if it's ever going to be, it's up to you. It is of utmost importance, therefore, to understand that your everyday decisions and actions will eventually create your actual future, in the process of time.

Someone once said, "We are born looking like our parents, but we will die looking like our decisions." Roy T. Bennett made a similar statement when he said, "You are not the victim of the world but rather the master of your own destiny. It is your choices and decisions that determine your destiny." Your decision to succeed, therefore, is one decision you must make. And only you can make it for yourself, no one else can make it for you if you are ever going to enjoy a rich and successful life. It will largely be dependent on your ability to make the right choices and decisions today. You can decide to go learn a new skill, change your career, go back to school, or even start your own business, etc. Whatever thing you want to accomplish in life will start the day that you decide to venture into it.

Noticed that I used the term venture, meaning it may be risky, difficult, or even impossible, but the day you make up your mind to go after it with a no-matter-what attitude, that's the day your life will change because all manner of support and circumstances you never thought that existed will begin to come to your aid.

I have personally experienced this mystery in my own personal life. When I was planning to relocate to the United States from my country, Nigeria, I literally did not know how it was going to happen, but I made a decision in my heart that it's time to try something new. The moment I made the decision to move the resources, finances, documentations, and personnel that are required for support, my dream began to sprang up from different sources, call it God, the supreme being, or the force of the universe. I discovered that the moment a man develops the will, power, and courage to go after whatever he desires, Providence move too.

In other words, your ability to make good decisions is one of the fundamental tools that you need to navigate through life successfully. Living beyond your limitations in life will oftentimes be depended on your ability to make good and definite decisions. Here is my point, your ability and willingness to be decisive rather than delay or procrastinate will put you in the fast track of your career and allows you to take total control of your life.

Motivational speaker and writer Anthony Robbins confirmed this when he said, "It is in your moment of decision that your life is shaped." The fact is that whenever you make a decision to work on something or to accomplish anything, whether it's to make good grades in school, get a new job, start a new career, or even to start your own business, unseen forces will come to your aid, bringing about assistance, support you never thought of and connections to see to the realization of that goal. Oftentimes we are faced with challenges that tries to limit us from taking the next step toward our desired goal in life. At such times, all we need to do is to believe in ourselves and take actions with courage. The most difficult thing is always the decision to act, but the moment you make the first decision and consistently act toward your desired goals with courage and tenacity, there is literally nothing that can stand on your way to the top.

"Once you decide to go after whatever you want in life, the universe conspires to make it happen," Ralph Waldo Emerson said. That is the power that lies in your ability to take a stand about whatever it is that you want to accomplish in life. When we look at the technology that we are enjoying today, it was as a result of some courageous decisions that was taken by people like me and you, people like Steve Jobs, Bill Gates, Mark Zuckerberg, etc. who all took courageous decisions to bring their dreams to actuality. And hence their contribution to the development of technology has dramatically transform the way we interact and communicate around the word today.

Take Facebook for example, through this media we can now share and exchange pictures and videos with our friends and love ones, not minding their location; we can even buy and market products on this simple platform, isn't that amazing? I bet it is. At some point, these inventions where merely thoughts in their hearts, but one thing made the difference: their decision and courage to act their God-given ideas. Imagine they never had the courage or the confidence to act on these ideas, we might not be enjoying what we are enjoying today.

So my question to you right now is what decision do you need to make about your life? What one step do you need to take that you are letting the fear of failure or what people will say withhold you from making? I want to challenge you to take that bold step today toward whatever it is that you want to accomplish. Because the moment you take a bold step toward it, the materials, resources, and the human support that you need to realize will begin to come your way.

I like the old English adage that says "Where there's a will, there's a way" is so true. All the good stuffs we are enjoying today were created by some set of individuals who had the will and courage to venture into their ideas. The airplanes, cars, even the chair you are sitting on right now was at some point an idea in someone's head. But they choose to act and believe in them that's why we have them today. If they were able to surmount all their limitations and turn their abstract ideas to reality, you, too, can bring yours to reality. But it's never going to happen for you unless you begin to take some courageous steps toward them. Unless you begin to take definite actions toward those ideas that pops into your mind on a daily basis. If it is ever going to happen, it is up to you. You have to act on life or risk life acting on you.

The fact is that there are opportunities everywhere, but you just have to open your eyes and take the first step in faith. It's so amazing how you take the first courageous step and the hand of God shows up to align you with the right circumstances, people, resources, and all manner of assistance to enable you reach your ultimate goal. But you just have to take the first step. Stop asking those limiting questions like, how am going to get resources, who is going to support me, what if my friends laugh at me, what if it doesn't work.

Apostle Paul made a very significant statement in the Book of Philippians 4:13 NKJV, "I can do all things to Christ that strengthens me." You have to wake up every morning and rephrase this word to yourself so many times throughout the day, "I can do all things through Christ that strengthens me." You have to realize that there is absolutely nothing you cannot accomplish once you have made a decision to go after it. Whatever dream or purpose you want to accomplish on your time on this earth, you have been equipped with the knowledge, abilities, and resources to reach them. But many of us never realize this because of lack of knowledge.

The Book of Hosea 4:6 confirmed this when it said, "My people perish for lack of knowledge." Noticed it didn't say lack of money, resources, or human support, rather it said lack of knowledge. In other words, all you need to move to the next level of your field and career is to discover the hidden capabilities, skills, and talent that God has deposited in you even before you were formed in your mother's womb. Because if you are not informed, you will be deformed, it's as simple as that.

The Scriptures advised in the Book of Proverbs 4:7, "Wisdom is the principal thing; therefore get wisdom: and with all thy getting get understanding." I wouldn't want to sound clairvoyant or super intelligent but let me submit to you that there is nothing you cannot accomplish if you decide and believe in yourself and consistently enhance your skills in whatever field or career you are into.

The truth is that you are well equipped with all the resources you may need to bring your dreams to lamplight by your heavenly Father. All you need right now is to say yes to your dreams and the possibilities that lies ahead of you.

I know that you might want to say, "But, Kennedy, you don't know my present condition, my background, my failures, my location, and my past." I know about all that, and I have experience them myself, but I choose not to let them stop me from rising to my greatest purpose in life; all those are what I call self-imposed limitations. All they do is to infuse our minds with negative thoughts that conversely fight to stop us from reaching our greater purpose in life; they tend to program our minds with fear that tries to limit us from moving forward. But you and I have to decide to see beyond those limitations. Because one fundamental lesson I have discovered over the years is that if you see beyond your limitations, you can live above them.

Author and speaker Anthony Robbins made a profound statement when he said, "More than anything else, I believe it's our decision, not the conditions of our lives, that determine our destiny." Understand that anybody on the second floor of a building was once at the first floor, any beautiful fruit you see on a tree was at some point a merely seed in the ground.

In other words, it makes no difference where you are right now in the pursuit of your dreams. All you need to do is to make a definite decision backed up with a commitment to rise to the ultimate purpose and calling of God upon your life. Think for a moment. Is there any difference between being interested in something and being committed to it? I bet there is. Oftentimes I hear some folks say things like, "I really would like to be rich," "I really like to graduate as the best student in my department," "I do really want to make a difference in the world," "I do really want to get back on shape, or be the best salesman in my company." But all this kind of statements are not commitment at all. They are simply wishing without commitment and effort to back them up.

Here is my point, until you would and should turn to a must, your level of accomplishment will be highly limited. You have to get committed to your dream and start working on it with faith. And you will not make any significant progress forward until you do. You have to decide today that no matter what life present to you, you will pursue your dream even if it goes all wrong, even if the stock market crashes, even if your lover leaves you, even if your family abandons you, even of no one gives you the support that you need. You still must be committed to your decision to live your dreams, at the highest level.

Understand that God has you in the palm of his hands, and if you don't give up on that dream, he has promised not to give up on you. He said, "I know the thoughts I think toward you, thoughts of peace and not of evil, thoughts to prosper you and give you the desires of your heart" (Jeremiah 29:11). God wants to take you to higher levels in your career, but it's left for you to make the decision to rise above your limiting beliefs.

I know some individuals who may say, "Well, I do like to decide like that, but I am not sure how I'm going to reach my dreams." The problem, however, is that they are paralyzed by their negative mental pictures, they are imprisoned by the fear of the past, fear of failure, fear of criticisms, fear of the unknown, etc., and this conversely hinders them from making the one important decision to go after their dreams. But I want you to understand that it is not important initially to know how you are going to create the result that you desire.

What is important, however, is to make the decision to take the first step in faith, and the way to accomplish all other things that are required will begin to show up. This may surprise you, but it is a proven fact that as soon as one truly commits to making something happen, the how to reach the pinnacle will reveal itself.

This simply means that whatever you hold strongly in your mind and continually act upon on a daily basis will eventually become a reality. Author and speaker Von Goethe went further to confirm this when he said, "Until one is committed, there is hesitancy, the chance to draw back, always ineffectiveness. Concerning all acts of initiative (and creation), there is one elementary truth, the ignorance of which kills countless ideas and splendid plans: that the moment one definitely commits oneself, then Providence moves too."

I want to challenge you to believe in yourself, decide today to never settle for less than you can be. Understand that the difference between you and the higher achievers in your field or career is simply because they are making better decisions than you are currently making. In other words, to get better results, you have to make better decisions.

However, to this extent, I wouldn't want to sound negative, but I do want to let you know that we are never going to experience a problem-free existence. It makes no difference how smart or intelligent you are, in as much as you are in the river of life, it's likely that you are going to hit a few roadblocks on your way to realizing whatever goal you have set for yourself. Hey, that doesn't mean I'm being negative, but I'm letting you know the factual truth.

Hence the key is when you run in the roadblocks and challenges of life, all you have to do is to beat yourself up and move on with your life. Remember that there are no failures anywhere in the world, there are only results. The fact that you failed does not make you a failure, it's only an indication that you have not succeeded yet. All you need, therefore, is to learn from the experience, observe your lapses, and make better decision in the future.

American actor Hannibal made a profound statement when he said, "You can either find a way or create one." You have to develop what I often call a no-matter-what attitude, an attitude that says yes even when there is every reason to say no, an attitude that says yes I can do it even when no one supports your dream, an attitude that persist in the means of difficulties and adversities. That's the kind of attitude that makes everything possible.

One of the most important decisions you can make to ensure your long-term happiness is to decide to use whatever life gives you at the moment to create what you want to see in the next moment. Author John L. Mason opined, "Use what you have at right there where you are." The truth of the matter is this, there is simply nothing you cannot do if you choose to focus all your time and abilities to it. It was Frank Tiger that says, "I know I cannot do everything, but I can do something, and I will not allow everything that I cannot do to stop me from doing that one thing that I can do."

The problem with many folks is that they drift through life without taking time to master one particular thing in their life. It is so amazing what we can accomplish if we take time to master and explore the many powers, skills, and abilities that lies dormant in us.

The human mind is designed to accomplish anything it set itself to accomplish. I want to challenge you today, here and now, to decide of whatever it is that you would like to accomplish. It makes no difference how impossible it may look from the unset or how lofty or difficult in may seem from your imagination. If you believe in it and give it all your time and focus, you will eventually bring it to actuality.

Yes, I know sometimes it may seem as if it's never going to happen. But one thing you must understand is that success and great accomplishment are never overnight experiences, it takes time and energy, it's a process of constant and continual action.

One of my greatest discovery is that oftentimes what seems impossible in the short term becomes very possible in the long term if you persist and refuse to give up. In other words, to truly succeed, we need to think long term. Success is processional, it is the small decisions and actions that eventually leads to huge success. You have to decide to persist until you see your dreams come true.

Understand that life is made up of seasons, and one exciting thing about the seasons of life is that none of them last forever. There is always going to be planting and harvesting time. The Scriptures confirmed this in the Book of Genesis 8:28, "As long the earth endures, seedtime and harvest, cold and heat, summer and winter, day and night will never cease." In other words, your decision and actions toward your desired goals are like seeds; as you take actions every day, you are simply sowing your seeds toward your desired future.

The fundamental lesson to note here is that if you persist in the means of challenges and setbacks—like the farmer also do during the planting season overcoming the weeds, rain, sun and even drought—you will eventually reap the rewards of your actions. It's, therefore, a matter of maintaining a constant and continual momentum toward your desired purpose.

The Scriptures encourage us in the Book of Psalms 30:5, "For his anger is but for a moment; his favor is for life; weeping may endure for a night, but joy comes in the morning." It's amazing what God can do in our life if we remain calm and steadfast to our purpose.

Understand that when you pass through diverse challenges and disappointments, he is just giving you a test to prove your faith in him and your level of belief and commitment to your dreams, and at such times all you need to do is to dig in your heels and say to yourself, "I will overcome, this too will pass, I can do all things through Christ that strengthens me, and I will persist until my dream becomes reality."

And if you stay in faith and continually reach out toward your goals, he has promise to give you the expectations of your heart. Therefore, I challenge you today to decide that your life will no longer be determine by your condition but by your decision and that you will not settle for less than you can be, then will your life to take on a new meaning and direction.

Key Important Points to Note from the Foregoing Chapter

1. It is not your present condition, location, or circumstances but your decision that will determine your ultimate destiny.
2. The moment that one decides to go after whatever him or her wishes to accomplish in life, the how to reach the pinnacle will begin to spring up from unexpected locations. That is the force available when you stake even your own existence to accomplish your heart's desires.
3. It is in your moment of decision that your ultimate destiny is shaped.
4. It is the small decisions and actions along the way that will eventually create your actual future. Therefore, the key is to maintain a constant and continual momentum even in the face of adversities and setbacks.

Principle Eleven

The Law of Attraction

You are a living magnet. You are invariably attracting to your life people and situations in harmony with your dominant thoughts.
—Brain Tracy

Everything you have in your life, you have attracted to yourself because of the way you think, the things you say, the pictures in your mind, and the things you expect. You can change your life by changing your thoughts, imaginations, and the things you say.

In other words, whatever results you are producing currently is simply a reflection of your dominant thoughts, be it negative or positive. For example, if you spend your time thinking about how people have treated you wrongly, how you have failed in the past, or how you are never going to succeed because of your past failures, you will invariably end up spending your days in resentment and negative imaginations which will in turn limit you from stepping into your goals with courage. And this will conversely lead you to producing negative results in your life. But if you turn your mind-set around and begin to do well on the positive events and situation around you and consistently maintain a positive mind-set, then the right circumstances will begin to manifest in your life and in everything you do.

Bob Proctor was right when he said, "If you see it in your mind, you will hold it in your hand." When I was planning to get in to college, I had a lot of limitations financially; my family was in a deep financial challenge. Our family business was affected by a government policy that led to the demolition of my family house. That event affected my parents and hindered them from providing money for my first-year tuition fee in college. My dad approached me and asked me to drop my dream of going to college and suggested that I should go and learn a trade instead or wait until things get back on track for the family financially. But I refused. I told him that my dream was to go to college, and I understood that he couldn't help me at that time, but I believed that God will make a way because he has promised to give me the desires of my heart.

I remained positive and kept praying for God's intervention. Most time when I'm alone in my room, I will visualize myself having all the resources that I needed to get into college, so I held that dream strong in my heart. I started behaving, dressing, and acting as if I'm in college already. One day I got a call from my uncle who lives in a different city. And after our discussion that day, he asked me to travel down to his city where he lives for a visit. So I left the next day to visit him. When I got there, he was so excited about my academic progress, and he promised to pay for my tuition fees not only for my first year but for my whole four years in college, and that was how my dream became a reality.

Now I narrated this story so you can understand truly how this law of attraction works. Noticed that I didn't have any money to pay for my tuition fee initially, but I had a dream and a belief that it was possible. And that conviction and mind-set sent a request to the universe that invariably attracted the financial assistance that I needed to make my dream a reality.

Here is my point, if it worked for me then, it can also work for you today. It makes no difference what your own goal or dream could be. If only you will stay in faith and maintain a positive mind-set, you will eventually attract the resources and connections that is required to make it a reality.

The Bible also confirmed this in the Book of Proverbs 23:7, "For as he thinket in his heart so is he." Have you ever observed thinking or talking about someone and within a few minutes your phone rings and you check the caller and surprisingly it turns out to be the person you were just thinking about? Now someone may say it's a coincidence, but it's not. That is a simple demonstration of the power of your thoughts. The moment you start thinking about anything consistently, your mind will send a signal to the universe to bring about your desire. Be it a dream vacation in Dubai, Paris, Hawaii or finding the right person to marry. The moment you understand how this principle works, it will literally transform the results in your life.

The fact is that you have the capacity to attract to yourself the most dominant thought in your heart. That's why you have to be conscious of what goes into your mind on a daily basis. Steve Jobs, the founder of Apple computers, literally did not initially know how he was going to bring his dream of making communication simpler and accessible the way it is today, but he conceived and believed in the idea and held it in his heart. Until he began to attract the materials, resources, and individuals that helped him bring his dream to reality. The fact is that it's not so important to understand how you are going to make your dream or idea come to reality. All you need, however, is the will to take the first step toward it, and the how to perfect it will gradually begin to spring up from different sources unknown to you.

You have to understand that whatever dream or purpose you want to fulfill was given to you by the supreme being, God. And he has already equipped you with the skills, potentials, and abilities to bring your dream to reality; all you need to do, therefore, is to believe in it without fear or doubt. You have to maintain a positive mind-set and stay in faith until you see it in actuality. God has already promised to give you the desires of your heart. But you have to consistently dominate your heart with beautiful and wonderful pictures of what you want to accomplish in your lifetime.

You have to get rid of doubts and fear and dominate your mind with possibilities and faith. You have to realize that that there is no limit to what you can accomplish. The fact is that the human spirit was not designed to observe limitation. We are the once that imposes limitations on our minds through our self-limiting beliefs.

Again the law of attraction can be understood by understanding that likes attract likes. What this means is that whether we realize it or not, we are responsible for bringing both negative and positive circumstances into our lives. Here is my point, when you consistently think positive and maintain an optimistic mind-set toward your goals, they will eventually become a reality.

In other words, expect good things to happen to you, not minding what is happening in your environment. Consistently imagine that you have unlimited potentials and that you can accomplish anything that you focus your mind to accomplish. Understand that your future is only limited by your own imagination, imagining that your greatest moments lie ahead and that everything that has happened to you up till now has merely prepared you for the greater things that lies ahead.

The truth is that when you expect good things to happen, good things usually happen to you. In the other hand, if you focus and expect negative things to happen, you are usually not disappointed. Your dominant thoughts and expectations have powerful influence over the outcome and the results in your life.

It was Joe Vitale that said, "It's really important that you feel good. Because this feeling good is what goes out as a signal into the universe and starts to attract more of itself to you. So the more you can feel good, the more you will attract the things that help you feel good and that will keep bringing you up higher and higher." You have to understand that where you place your focus on will negatively or positively influence your life. Your thoughts, affirmations, visualization, and expectation are all very important tools used by the law of attraction to attract whatever you want in life.

I discovered very early in life that whatever you consistently think and affirm, you will become. I remember my years of growing up as a teenager about seventeen years ago. I often tell my friends that I will travel to America one day to further my education, and they will argue sometimes and ask how I'm going to get the resources to make that possible. But I will always respond to them, "I don't know how it's going to happen, but I do would love to travel there one day." I consistently confess and held that idea in my head.

Most times when I'm alone, I will visualize myself, chatting and playing with white people, and that built my faith over time, and I started working toward it. Over the years things work out for me, and the opportunity came. So I grabbed it. And today as I'm writing this book, I have already spent two and half years in America. That dream came to pass. Now that's the law of attraction. One of the most fundamental discovery of human existence.

Author and speaker Napoleon Hill rightly confirmed this when he said, "You become what you think most of the time." In other words, where you are right now is as a result of your thoughts and belief about what is possible, and if you want to see a better you and a more prosperous you in the years to come, you may have to start thinking and believing that you can accomplish whatever dream you have set for yourself.

If you consistently use words like, I'm rich, I'm prosperous, I'm the best, I'm a winner, it will begin to take solid root in your subconscious mind and start reflecting in everything you do. That's the power of the human spirit, you are like a living magnet; whatever you consistently talk about and focus on will eventually come to you. "All that we are is as a result of what we have thought" (Buddha).

In other words, your outer world is a reflection of your inner world. It makes no difference whether it is positive or negative. It all boils down to the capacity of your mind because whatever you can vividly imagine in your mind, you can bring it to actuality. I want to encourage you to nurture your mind with positive and productive thoughts because you can never go higher than your thoughts. Again stay away from negative-minded people, they will always try to belittle your ambition; instead hang around with people who are dreamers and positive minded, they will help expand your vision of yourself and help you realize your greatest potentials.

Focus your mind on the positive things of life. Understand that you are the prophet of your own destiny. If you spend your days wallowing about the failures of the past or about the fear of the future, you will likely to see more negative situations appearing in your life. But if you focus and think about what is good and the opportunities that lies ahead, then you will soon start seeing the right circumstances and events surrounding you.

Therefore, the law of attraction encourages you to see and understand that you have the powers within you to create the kind of life and experience that you want to have at any point in your life. You can decide to change the events of your life by changing your dominant thoughts and visualization.

You can shape your future and the kind of people that comes into your life by taking charge of your thoughts, it's as simple as that. When you learn how to use the many powerful tools that are associated with the law of attraction, you will start thinking in a more optimistic and positive way, then you will start attracting the right circumstances and events into your life.

For example, using the visualization tool. You are encouraged to spend ten to fifteen minutes on meditating and visualizing positive images of what you want to see in your preferable future, who you want to be, what you want to have, how much you want to make, where you want to travel to, whatever it is that you desire to have; just focus all your thoughts and imagination in creating them, and in the process of time, you will begin to attract them into your life.

Secondly we can also use the tool of affirmation. Using this tool, I encouraged you to consistently say and talk about positive, productive, and excellent things that you want to see and experience in your life. You might not have realized it before now, but the earth itself was created by spoken words.

The Bible confirmed this in Genesis 1:1–14. Verse 3 of that chapter reads, "And God said, 'Let there be light' and there was light." Noticed that it didn't say God created or God crafted, rather it accounts that God said let there be light, and immediately there was light. Here you see the power of affirmation displayed.

Again the Bible recorded that we are made in God's image. In other words, we can do the same things he did in his time on earth. What that means, therefore, is that you can begin to chart the course of your own life using your confessions on a daily basis. You can have whatsoever you say; your words are like seeds that will eventually germinate in your future. You have to consistently speak things that are in harmony with what you want to be, have, and accomplish in your life.

For example, when someone approaches you and ask you how you are doing, your response should not reflect what you are feeling at that particular time, rather it should reflect the way you want to feel in the next moment. In other words, stop confessing what you are seeing in your life right now and start confessing what you want to see in your future, and I recommend you use words like, I'm doing great, I'm doing wonderful, I'm making massive progress. It makes no difference how you are feeling right now. Make it a lifestyle to only confess what you want to see and not what is happening at the moment because you will eventually reap the confessions of your mouth, be it negative or positive.

It makes no difference what is happening around you or how your past experiences have shaped your life. You can choose right now to chart a new cause for your life by speaking out the positive things that you want to see in your life, visualizing the right circumstances, and dominating your mind with the right mental pictures. Your thoughts are like a living magnet, you will eventually attract to yourself what you think about most of the time. You may have come from a very poor background and maybe you were not able to get a good education or learn any lucrative skill, but you don't have to let that determine the rest of your life, instead decide to get yourself back on track.

Author and speaker Les Brown made a profound statement when he said, "It's never too late to dream a new dream." I suggest you start hanging around positive-minded people, people that will expand your mind to see the possibility that lies ahead of you. Start reading positive materials like the Bible, inspirational books, and listen to self-uplifting audio massages that will expand your mental capacity.

You might have failed in so many ventures or experienced some disappointment in the past. You have to get them off your mind and move on; stop dowelling on them and start dominating your heart with positive thoughts, thoughts like, my better days are still ahead of me, I'm highly favored and blessed by my heavenly Father, all things are still going to work out for my good, I can do all things through Christ who strengthens me.

When you begin to program your mind with thoughts like this, it will begin to align your life with the right situation and circumstances. Things will begin to fall in place again for you, and you will eventually begin to attract the right kind of people into your life. Henry Ford was right when he said, "Whether you think you can or you think you cannot, you are right." As a man thinks, so he is. Change your thinking, change your life.

Key Important Points to Note from the Foregoing Chapter

1. Literally all the things you have in your life right now, you have attracted to yourself through your thoughts and beliefs about what is possible for you, but the good news is that you can turn things around by thinking differently.
2. Understand that your words are like seeds. You have to be mindful of what you say because they will eventually germinate in your future. Be it positive or negative.
3. Whatever you can conceive in your heart, with a strong conviction, you will eventually become, think big.
4. Hang around positive-minded people, read inspirational books, and consistently listen to positive audio massages.

Principle Twelve

Take Action

Act on life or risk life acting on you.

It has been a great journey thus far, and I'm excited about the opportunity to have shared some of my stories and life principles with you. I believe that you have been able to shake off some of the self-imposed limitations that has been stopping you from taking action on your dreams. Now I want to challenge you to stop putting off what you can do today until tomorrow.

    American philosopher William James stressed, "The essence of education is not knowledge but action." At this point, I want to challenge you to start taking bold steps toward your dreams. One of the highest killer of a man's dream is procrastination. Oftentimes I hear people make statements like, I will do it when the snow goes away, I will do it tomorrow, I will do it when the sun comes down or when its stops raining.

    The fact is that there is never going to be a perfect time to act on your dream. The Book of Ecclesiastics 11:4 TLB has this to say, "If you wait for perfect condition, you will never get anything done." You have to understand that your time is your most valuable resources. The fact is that your dream cannot become a reality until you start acting on them. So I want to recommend to you these five tested-and-proven steps that will avail you the required motivation to start acting on your dreams and improving your personal life.

Step 1: I want you to write down four actions you need to take that you have been putting off. Maybe you need to meet up with a new prospective partner for your business, maybe you need to go back to school, maybe you need to lose some weight, maybe you need to reconnect with someone important to you, etc.

Step 2: I want you to write down all the reasons why you have not taken action toward each and every one of those goals that you have set out for yourself, and I want you to be honest with yourself about these reasons.

Step 3: I want you to start brainstorming yourself about all the rewards and benefits that you will eventually realize by acting on your goal.

Step 4: I want you to write down what it will ultimately cost you in the long run if you don't decide to act on your goals today, if you don't make that phone call, if you don't start consistently working out each day, if you don't go back to school. Be honest with yourself. What will this decision cost you over the next say two, three, four, five years from now? What is going to cost you emotionally? What is going to cost you in terms of your own self-image? What will it cost you in terms of your physical appearance? What will it cost you in your feeling of self-esteem? What will it cost you financially? What will it cost you in your relationship with people that you love the most? Now when you're put all these facts in consideration, do you see the more reason why you should act on your goals, or are you still going to keep on wallowing in mediocrity and procrastination rather than taking charge of your destiny? The choice is yours.

Step 5: Write down all the pleasure that you will enjoy by taking each of these actions right now, and I want you to make a huge list that will give you the excitement and motivation to take action.

I want to encourage you to take the time to complete this exercise and to take the advantage of the great momentum that you have been building up as you have moved through this book. Understand that the only thing that can stop you from moving forward is you.

In conclusion, I want you to make it a rule of life that you will never again settle for less than you can become and that you will stick to that dream until you see it becomes reality. I look forward to meeting you and hearing the story of your life success. Till then. Remember that if you don't give up, God will not give up on you. Step out in courage, there are no limit to your potentials.

Reference and Resources

(Where Did You Get Your Information?)

1. AWAKEN THE GIANT WITHIN, BY ANTHONY ROBBINS. PAGES 199, 236, 242.
2. LEAVE YOUR DREAMS. BY LESS BROWN. PAGES 22, 98,
3. PASTOR TOMMY TOMMY… SERMON ON LAWS OF LIFE. 19/2/2006
4. SUBJECTIVE IDEALISM. FINAL YEAR THESIS BY MYSELF,… KENNEDY KING. PAGES 78, 98, 211.
5. THE OXFORD ADVANCE LEARNERS DICTIONARY.& THE NEW KING JAMES VERSION OF TH BIBLE.
6. QUOTES BY JOHN MASON… GOOGLE SEARCH.
7. QUOTES BY JOHN C, MAXWELL, GOOGLE SEARCH
8. QUOTES BY NAPOLEON HILL, GOOGLE SEARCH.
9. QUOTES BY ARISTOTLE,… GOOGLE SEARCH.

About the Author

Kennedy K. Odimba is the president and founder of King's Solutions Network, a social media platform that is set up to inspire individuals to live up to their full potentials and maximize every hidden greatness within them.

He holds a bachelor's degree in philosophy from Imo State University and a proficiency certification in management. He is currently pursuing his second degree in computer science at the prestigious Nashville State Community College in Tennessee, United States.

He is a seasoned motivational speaker and a peak performance consultant with Isagenix, a wellness and a nutritional company that is helping individuals to rejuvenate their health and financial goals.

He presently residing in Nashville, Tennessee, with his son, Brandon U. Odimba.

My Facebook: Kennedy King
My Facebook Page: King's Solutions Network
My Instagram: KENNEDYKING450
Phone: 6158567422

Please be sure to visit my YouTube Channel:
King's Solution Network at:
https://www.youtube.com/channel/UCfbjRUVBScZC03A7Ozz0fuw

CPSIA information can be obtained
at www.ICGtesting.com
Printed in the USA
JSHW021400100520
5551JS00001B/2